THE SHOOTING SCRIPT

ARARAT

THE SHOOTING SCRIPT

ARARAT

SCREENPLAY AND INTRODUCTION BY
ATOM EGOYAN

AFTERWORD BY
TIMOTHY TAYLOR

A Newmarket Shooting Script® Series Book
NEWMARKET PRESS • NEW YORK

FIRST EDITION

02   03   04   10   9   8   7   6   5   4   3   2   1

ISBN: 1-55704-552-6 (paperback)

Library of Congress Cataloging-in-Publication Data is available upon request.

QUANTITY PURCHASES

Companies, professional groups, clubs, and other organizations may qualify for special terms when ordering quantities
of this title. For information, write to Special Sales, Newmarket Press, 18 East 48th Street, New York, NY 10017;
call (212) 832-3575 or 1-800-669-3903; FAX (212) 832-3629; or e-mail mailbox@newmarketpress.com.

Website: www.newmarketpress.com

Manufactured in the United States of America.

OTHER BOOKS IN THE NEWMARKET SHOOTING SCRIPT® SERIES INCLUDE:

The Age of Innocence: The Shooting Script
American Beauty: The Shooting Script
A Beautiful Mind: The Shooting Script
The Birdcage: The Shooting Script
Blackhawk Down: The Shooting Script
Cast Away: The Shooting Script
Dead Man Walking: The Shooting Script
Erin Brockovich: The Shooting Script
Gods and Monsters: The Shooting Script
Gosford Park: The Shooting Script
Human Nature: The Shooting Script
The Ice Storm: The Shooting Script
Knight's Tale: The Shooting Script

Man on the Moon: The Shooting Script
The Matrix: The Shooting Script
Nurse Betty: The Shooting Script
The People vs. Larry Flynt: The Shooting Script
The Shawshank Redemption: The Shooting Script
Red Dragon: The Shooting Script
Snatch: The Shooting Script
Snow Falling on Cedars: The Shooting Script
State and Main: The Shooting Script
Traffic: The Shooting Script
The Truman Show: The Shooting Script
U-Turn: The Shooting Script

OTHER NEWMARKET PICTORIAL MOVIEBOOKS AND NEWMARKET INSIDER FILM BOOKS INCLUDE:

The Age of Innocence: A Portrait of the Film★
Ali: The Movie and the Man★
Amistad: A Celebration of the Film by Steven Spielberg
The Art of The Matrix★
Bram Stoker's Dracula: The Film and the Legend★
Cradle Will Rock: The Movie and the Moment★
Crouching Tiger, Hidden Dragon: A Portrait of the Ang Lee Film★
Dances with Wolves: The Illustrated Story of the Epic Film★
E. T. The Extra Terrestrial From Concept to Classic—The Illustrated
    Story of the Film and the Filmmakers
Frida: Bringing Frida Kahlo's Life and Art to Film
Gladiator: The Making of the Ridley Scott Epic Film

The Jaws Log
Men in Black: The Script and the Story Behind the Film★
Neil Simon's Lost in Yonkers: The Illustrated Screenplay of the Film★
Planet of The Apes: Re-imagined by Tim Burton★
Saving Private Ryan: The Men, The Mission, The Movie
The Sense and Sensibility Screenplay & Diaries★
The Seven Years in Tibet Screenplay and Story★
Stuart Little: The Art, the Artists and the Story Behind the Amazing
    Movie★
Windtalkers: The Making of the Film About the Navajo Code Talkers
    of World War II

★Includes Screenplay

CONTENTS

INTRODUCTION

BY ATOM EGOYAN

At the press conference for *The Sweet Hereafter* at Cannes in 1997, a journalist asked me if the film couldn't be seen as a metaphor for the Armenian Genocide. It was one of the few times in my life when I found myself quite speechless. The journalist went on to suggest that many of my films had dealt with themes of denial and its consequences, and was interested as to why I hadn't dealt with the subject more directly.

It was a good question.

I should begin with some personal facts. My grandparents from my father's side were victims of the horrors that befell the Armenian population of Turkey in the years around 1915. My grandfather, whose entire family save his sister was wiped out in the massacres, married my grandmother who was the sole survivor of her family. I never knew either of these people. They had both died long before I was born.

When my parents moved to Canada, they settled in Victoria—a city on the west coast where we were the only Armenian family. Though Armenian was my mother tongue, I was desperate to assimilate. Although I sometimes heard stories of what the Turks had done to my grandparents, I certainly wasn't raised with anger or hatred. I was too concerned with trying to be like all the other kids to dwell on these ancient grievances.

I left home at eighteen to study classical guitar and international relations in Toronto. At the university, there was an active Armenian Students' Association, and I was exposed to an Armenian community for the first time. It's important to understand this was an extremely crucial moment in the evolution of Armenian politics. Armenian terrorists (or "freedom fighters," depending on your point of view) were beginning their systematic attacks against Turkish figures. Many Turkish ambassadors and consuls were being assassinated in this period, as Armenians extremists were enraged by the continued Turkish denial of what their grandparents had suffered.

I was completely torn by these events. While one side of me could understand the rage that informed these acts, I was also appalled by the cold-blooded nature of these killings. I was fascinated by what it would take for a person who was raised and educated with North American values of tolerance to get involved with these acts. One of the first feature scripts I ever wrote dealt with this issue.

Thankfully, I never made that film. At that point, twenty years ago, I wasn't ready to deal with the "Armenian Issue."

The problem with any film that deals with the "Armenian Issue," is that there are so many issues to deal with. First of all, there's the historical event. Since no widely-released dramatic movie had ever presented the genocide, it was important that any film project would need to show what happened. We live in a popular culture that demands images before we allow ourselves to believe, and it would be unimaginable to deal with this history without presenting what the event looked like.

I believe that the most dramatic aspect of this history, however, is not the way it happened, but how it's been denied. Since the end of World War I, Turkey has refused to acknowledge the Genocide, going so far as to claim that it was in fact Armenians who committed genocide against the Turks. While this may seem preposterous, it is important to remember that there is now a generation of Turks who have been raised with this denial. They aren't denying anymore. It's what they've been led to believe.

From the moment I began to write this script, I was drawn to the idea of what it means to tell a story of horror. In this case, the horror isn't only about the historical events that took place in Turkey over eighty-five years ago, but also the enduring horror of living with something so cataclysmic that has been systematically denied. Without getting into the mechanics of that denial (there are a number of books and articles on that issue), it is important to note that the role of the director in my film-within-the-film is monumental. Edward Saroyan, and his screenwriter, Rouben, are faced with an awesome task. They will be the first filmmakers to present these images to a wide public. If their film seems raw and blunt in its depictions, it's because they are the first people to cinematically present these "unspeakable horrors." They are desperate to get the point across.

We learn that Edward's mother was a survivor of the genocide—that he is making this film to honour her spirit. Needless to say, such noble personal intentions do not necessarily lend themselves to critical distance, and it's clear from the glimpses we see of Edward's movie that it might sometimes veer into an exaggerated and extreme view of history. Like many epics, it paints its heroes and its villains in an "over-the-top" way in order to heighten the sense of drama. Edward's *Ararat* is a sincere attempt to show what happened, told from the point of view of a boy who was raised with these images by his mother—a genocide survivor. The scenes of the film-within-the-film represent the way many survivors and children who were told of these horrors would recall these events.

I decided to create this film-within-the-film in order to generate the drama in the present day. All of the central characters in my *Ararat* are somehow connected to the making of Edward's *Ararat*, and most of the conflicts that occur in the contemporary story are related to the unresolved nature of not only the genocide, but also the difficulties and compromises faced by the representation of this atrocity. How does an artist speak the unspeakable? What does it mean to listen? What happens when it is denied?

These are hugely complicated issues, and I certainly have enormous expectations of my viewer. While my work may have been different if a more popular movie version of the Armenian Genocide had already existed, this was not the case. Thus the screenplay had to tell the story of what happened, why it happened, why it's denied, why it continues to happen, and what happens when you continue to deny. *Ararat* is a story about the transmission of trauma. It is cross-cultural and inter-generational. The grammar of the screenplay uses every possible tense available, from the past, present, and future, to the subjective and the conditional. I firmly believe that this was the only way the story could be told. It is dense and complicated because the issues are so complex.

In comparing the shooting script to the final version of the film, a few key scenes are missing. First of all, there was an attempt to thread the symbol of Mount Ararat into the David-Philip-Ali story to parallel its appearance in the Armenian characters' lives (Scene 7). This seemed to make sense, since Ararat is both a national symbol to Armenians, as well as the biblical mountain where Noah's ark landed and is thus—by extension—a symbol to which we are all somehow connected. While this seemed to be an interesting literary idea, it seemed forced and highly contrived in the first edited version of the film.

David's comment about Noah taking "two of every kind" and his grandson's subsequent question about not taking any "gay animals" were amusing, but they seemed to set the film off on the wrong tone. Indeed, the ultimate repetition of the Noah and the ark story by Philip to his son (he tries to disprove David's comments by bringing in the story of the Unicorn) seemed to be an unnecessary convolution in the first cut of the film, as was Ali's final conversation with his lover's son about their lifestyle (Scenes 63-64).

I was hesitant about making Philip and Ali gay, since it seemed to raise so many other issues that weren't essential to the story. Ultimately, however, it seemed the most economical way of finding a conflict between David and his son that would have resonance and repercussions throughout the rest of the story. In terms of the inter-generational theme, the idea that Philip would be so paranoid of his father's judgmental attitude against his life choice that he threatens to block David's access to his grandson was powerful. This is what happens in families. People make irrational and extreme decisions based on personal insecurities. The internal intolerance which can destroy a family is not so different from the institutional intolerance which can destroy a race.

Also, I found it profound that Ali—raised in a culture that would strongly disapprove of his homosexuality—could be so comfortable as a gay Turkish man. The fact that he is initially presented as someone so at ease in his skin makes it all the more dramatic that he becomes so uncomfortable with himself once he portrays the stereotypical Turkish monster in Edward's film. It was important that Ali—though a supporting character in the screenplay—emerges as a hugely important role in the film. He is a Turkish character who has been raised with no knowledge of the Armenian genocide. While the Jevdet Bey character he plays in Edward's film is certainly evil (and based on a true figure), Ali's presence asks the viewer to consider whether we can judge people today for actions taken long ago by people who are no longer present.

The second major cut was the scene between Ani and Gorky, spoken in Armenian, about his ghost being raised as a dramatic figure in Edward's film (Scene 62). I always loved this moment, even though I'm not a usual fan of such "magic realism." In the first cut, however, it seemed to completely break the spell of Gorky's remarkable incarnation in the film. While having Ani walk onto Edward's set to interrupt Martin's scenery-chewing monologue was effective, it seemed redundant to repeat this gesture a few scenes later.

•   •   •

There is an alchemy that a performance creates that can never be anticipated by the screenplay. While the Arshile Gorky studio scenes have an expository and matter-of-fact quality in the scenario, the visual effect of seeing the painting gradually come to life was much more emotionally loaded on the screen. Indeed, Gorky—as the most famous survivor of the Armenian Genocide—came to represent the spirit of this horror. More than any of Edward's extreme representations of atrocity, the painting of *The Artist and His Mother* emerges as the most profound artistic expression of loss and unspeakable suffering. The moment where Gorky rubs his mother's hands from the canvas is the closest we come to understanding the spiritual desecration of genocide, as well as the power of art to help heal such pain.

Thus, to have the ghost of Gorky suddenly appear to Ani in a Pirandellian moment of self-deconstruction seemed to diminish his powerful presence in the film. In a film which tries to carefully harness the cause and effect of storytelling and narrative, this final comment by a historical character on his own fictional representation in the movie seemed to border on the ridiculous. While there is certainly a temptation to explain and defend every decision, it goes a little too far when a screen character shifts into auto-critique!

At the very last moment, I added the idea that Raffi would read Siamanto's poem, *The Dance*, to the customs officer as a way of framing this account (Scenes 67-70). I was suddenly struck by the fact that this famous poem—written by a writer who was murdered in 1915—was told through the distancing device of a third person account. A German woman who has watched the torture and immolation of Armenian young women tells the story of the burning "brides" to the writer. This poem is then re-told by the screenwriter, Rouben, which is then interpreted by the actors directed by Edward. Raffi watches this scene being shot, then re-tells the story—which he witnesses as a constructed scene—to a complete stranger, David. The layers of transfer and reception are complex, but absolutely necessary as the story shifts from the eyewitness, to the epistolary, to the dramatized, and finally back to the eyewitness.

History is not only the responsibility of the person who speaks the truth. It needs someone to listen. *When* that person listens, *how* they listen, *why* they listen are all essential components of the communication of experience. While the structure of *Ararat* is densely layered with these issues, I needed to show how the collective human linkage of action and responsibility is both the wonder and tragedy of our condition.

I couldn't have made this film any other way.

ARARAT

a true story about living proof

A film
by
Atom Egoyan

Final Shooting Script

April 2001

Ararat

1   INT. ARSHILE GORKY'S STUDIO. NYC 1935 -- DAY

An old black and white photo of a boy and his mother. The
mother is seated, her hands on her lap. The young boy is
standing beside her, holding some flowers in his hand.

The camera pulls out from this emotionally loaded photograph
to reveal an artist's desk.

Extreme close-ups of a pencil beginning to copy the details
of this photograph onto a piece of paper.

Title credits are superimposed over this sequence, sensually
depicting the process of one medium being transformed into
another.

                                                   CUT TO:

2   EXT. TORONTO AIRPORT. CUSTOMS STATION -- DAY

A haunting, blurry image of exhausted people marching across
a desert. As the camera weaves through this dreamlike sight,
the rags and torn clothing of this destitute crowd is
gradually transformed into the suits and modern attire of a
line waiting for passport inspection at an airport.

The camera finds the face of EDWARD, an elegant man in his
early seventies. He speaks with a French accent.

                                                   CUT TO:

3   INT. TORONTO AIRPORT. CUSTOMS STATION -- DAY

EDWARD is standing in front of DAVID, a customs officer in
his sixties.

DAVID is holding a pomegranate that he has found in EDWARD's
bag.

                         DAVID
              You can't bring this in.

                         EDWARD
              Please.

                         DAVID
              No fruits or vegetables. That
              includes pomegranates. It's on your
              form.

                    EDWARD
          Let me explain. I like to eat the
          seeds of this fruit. One each day.
          For luck.

                    DAVID
          I'm sorry. It's not allowed.

EDWARD extracts a small knife from his pocket. He cuts open
the pomegranate on the table.

                    DAVID (CONT'D)
          What are you doing?

                    EDWARD
          This way, I don't need to bring it
          in. I will eat it here. At the
          gate of your country. Look...

Using his knife, EDWARD pries the pomegranate open, extracts
some seeds, and puts them in his mouth.

                    EDWARD (CONT'D)
          I'll bring the luck in my stomach.
          Would you like some?

DAVID smiles at EDWARD, and shakes his head.

                                              CUT TO:

4   INT. TORONTO AIRPORT. ARRIVALS DOOR -- DAY

EDWARD leaves the baggage area. He is met by a production
assistant.

                    ASSISTANT
          Mr. Saroyan. Welcome...

EDWARD raises his fingers to his mouth, from which he expels
a handful of pomegranate seeds he has smuggled in.

                    EDWARD
          Where can I put these?

                                              CUT TO:

5   INT. UNIVERSITY LECTURE HALL -- DAY

A slide image of the photograph of the mother and son seen
at the beginning of the film. This slide image dissolves
into another slide image of the drawing inspired from this
photograph.

> ANI
> (voice-over)
> ...while it's obvious to see the
> evolution from photograph, to sketch,
> to the final painting, there is
> another essential layer...

The drawing of the slide dissolves to a slide of Arshile
Gorky's painting, 'The Artist and His Mother'. It is inspired
from the photograph that was seen at the beginning of the
film. The slide switches to an image of a beautiful lake,
mountains in the background.

ANI, early-forties, is giving a lecture to the students of
her art history class.

> ANI (CONT'D)
> The painter, Arshile Gorky, was born
> in a village on the shores of Lake
> Van...

ANI switches the slide to an image of Aghtamar, an ancient
Armenian church on an island in Lake Van.

> ANI (CONT'D)
> From the shores of this village, the
> island of Aghtamar was in plain view.
> As a child, Gorky would travel to
> this island with his mother, who
> would show him the detailed carvings
> on the walls of the church.

ANI switches the slide to a stone image of Madonna and Child
on the wall of this church.

> ANI (CONT'D)
> While Gorky's famous self portrait
> has been compared to Cezanne and
> Picasso, I believe its true
> inspiration can be traced to this
> magnificent carving...

The slide switches to Gorky's masterpiece, The Artist and
His Mother.

ANI pauses as she notices someone in the class.

CELIA is an attractive young woman in her mid-twenties.
While the other students are busy taking notes, CELIA stares
back at ANI.

CELIA is not supposed to be there. There is tension between
the two women.

CUT TO:

6   INT. STUDIO. MISSION SET -- DAY

EDWARD walking through the partially constructed set of a
fortified mission compound. He is followed by ROUBEN, an
intense looking man in his late-forties, and MARTIN, a
handsome leading man.

                    EDWARD
          For many years, I felt I could not
          tell this story.

                    MARTIN
          Why not?

                    ROUBEN
          Because the Armenian Genocide has no
          resolution. The Turkish government
          has never admitted their crime, so
          it's like a story without an end.

MARTIN stares at ROUBEN. He didn't ask him to respond.
EDWARD stops in front of a group of painters hoisting a huge
representation of Mount Ararat on the studio wall.

                    EDWARD
          Mount Ararat. When I was a boy, my
          mother used to tell me this was ours,
          even though it was so far away. I
          used to dream of a way to approach
          it, to make it belong to who I
          was...to who I became. Will this
          film bring us closer?

                    MARTIN
               (slight smile)
          I guess that depends on how good a
          job we do.

                    ROUBEN
          Marty...
               (ROUBEN presents a
               book to MARTIN)
          This book is the key to your
          character. It's the actual journal
          of Clarence Ussher, published in
          Boston in 1917. He was a missionary,
          an American doctor who witnessed the
          whole thing.
                    (MORE)

ROUBEN (CONT'D)
Every scene in my script is based on
this document. It's a true story
about a man who saw an entire
community wiped out. So you can't--
you can't play him like he's just a
guy doing a job...

MARTIN stares unnervingly at ROUBEN.

ROUBEN (CONT'D)
Is that at all...useful...?

MARTIN
(with an edge)
You want me to act.

ROUBEN
No, I'm just saying...

ROUBEN stares at MARTIN, lost for words. EDWARD is at a
distance, staring at the huge image of Ararat.

MARTIN
(to ROUBEN, holding
the book)
I've read this book, as well as every
piece of archival material, every
word that so much as hints at this
region, these people, or the Armenian
genocide. I'm currently re-reading
the Holy Bible, with my character,
Clarence Ussher, in mind. Beyond
all this, it's pretty much up to my
imagination.

MARTIN observes a short dramatic pause. ROUBEN is stunned
into silence.

MARTIN (CONT'D)
Now, I'm here to make a film with
Edward Saroyan.

MARTIN points at EDWARD, then approaches him, leaving ROUBEN
alone.

EDWARD
(to MARTIN, full of
emotion)
This was the mountain my mother never
saw after her family was destroyed.
(MORE)

                              EDWARD (CONT'D)
              Butchered in front of her eyes.
              Ararat was her dream. This is my
              gift to her spirit.

                                                        CUT TO:

7   INT. ALI'S APARTMENT. LIVING/DINING AREA -- DAY

        TONY, five, has just opened a birthday present from his
        grandfather. It is a toy of Noah's Ark. DAVID shows his
        grandson how to work it. There is a wooden plank which leads
        the animals into the ark.

                              DAVID
              You put the animals on
              this...plank...up they go. Two by
              two.

        PHILIP, early forties, watches this scene. He is TONY's
        father and DAVID's son. He has his arm around his younger
        boyfriend, ALI.

                              PHILIP
              What do you say to Grandpa?

                              TONY
              Thank you, Grandpa.

                              DAVID
              You're very welcome, Tony.

                              TONY
              Grandpa, what do you mean, 'two by
              two'?

        DAVID avoids eye contact with his son PHILIP, who keeps his
        arm around ALI. All his attention is focused on TONY.

                              DAVID
                   (guarded)
              Well...one male and one female.

        PHILIP looks at ALI, feeling he must say something. But
        before he can speak, TONY asks...

                              TONY
                   (confused)
              Didn't Noah take gay animals?

                                                        CUT TO:

8   EXT. JANET'S HOUSE -- DAY

PHILIP has pulled up in front of a modest house in a decent
neighborhood. ALI is in the front seat beside him. DAVID
and TONY are having a conversation at the back.

                    TONY
          Is the ark still there?

                    DAVID
          Well, they went to look for it on
          Mount...Ararat...a few years ago,
          but they didn't find anything.

                    TONY
          Does that mean it isn't real?

                    DAVID
          No, just that...they didn't look in
          the right place.

PHILIP is impatient with his father.

                    PHILIP
          Do you want to take him in?

                    DAVID
          Of course.

DAVID takes his young grandson out of the car and approaches
the house as PHILIP and ALI watch.

                    ALI
              (sarcastic)
          You're right. It was a great idea
          to invite your Dad over for his
          birthday.

                    PHILIP
          What the fuck was I thinking?

ANGLE ON

The door of the house is opened by an attractive woman in
her thirties.

                    DAVID
          Hello, Janet.

DAVID and JANET embrace. There is a warmth and affection
between them. TONY is pleased to see this. The little boy
hugs the legs of his grandfather and mother.

ANGLE BACK ON

PHILIP and ALI watching this 'family hug' from the distance
of the car.

                    ALI
          I thought you said they didn't get
          along.

                    PHILIP
          They don't.

                                        CUT TO:

9   INT. ANI'S HOUSE. FRONT ROOM. -- NIGHT

ANI is having a dinner party. There is a boisterous
conversation in Armenian, full of laughter and jokes.

RAFFI, ANI's son, is also seated in the living room. He is
a handsome, brooding young man in his early twenties. The
doorbell rings. RAFFI moves to answer it. It's CELIA.

                    RAFFI
          Hi.

The moment ANI spots CELIA at the door, she springs up and
leaves her guests, who continue their hearty argument in
Armenian. RAFFI dreads this confrontation.

                    CELIA
               (with an edge)
          Hi, Mom.

                    ANI
          What were you doing in my class?

                    CELIA
          I thought I'd drop by.

                    ANI
          Why?

CELIA pauses a beat, then...

                    CELIA
          Curiosity.

                    RAFFI
          Let's go.

                    ANI
          Aren't you going to say goodbye?

RAFFI moves away from the two women to say goodbye to the guests in Armenian as CELIA and ANI stare at each other.

> ANI (CONT'D)
> (to CELIA)
> Since when have you been curious
> about what I do?

> CELIA
> I've always been very curious about
> what you do.
> (beat)
> And what you've done.

CUT TO:

10   EXT. WAREHOUSE.   FIRE ESCAPE -- NIGHT

CELIA and RAFFI walk towards a warehouse in an industrial part of town.   They are in the middle of a conversation.

> RAFFI
> You can't show up in her class without
> letting her know.

> CELIA
> No?

> RAFFI
> You need permission.

> CELIA
> Why?

> RAFFI
> It's the rules.

> CELIA
> I think we're a little beyond rules.

CUT TO:

11   INT. WAREHOUSE -- NIGHT

CELIA lives in a large loft space.   In one corner is a hydroponic marijuana farm.   The lush greens of the plants are in stark contrast to naked lightbulbs dangling from the ceiling.

The loft is strewn with a collection of eclectic art, some of it found, some of it made.   A computer occupies another corner of the space.

RAFFI is playing violin. CELIA is spritzing the plants with water.

> CELIA
> Why can't I read her book?

RAFFI tries to keep concentrated on his violin playing.

> RAFFI
> Wait till it comes out.

> CELIA
> You've read it.

> RAFFI
> Sure.

> CELIA
> Give me your copy.

> RAFFI
> No.

> CELIA
> Why not?
> (smiling)
> I'm part of the family.

> RAFFI
> I promised her...
> (he hesitates)

> CELIA
> What?

> RAFFI
> That I wouldn't give you my copy.

CELIA moves over to RAFFI, beginning to get playful.

> CELIA
> (like a girl)
> Aw, please...

> RAFFI
> Celia...

CELIA stares at RAFFI, her eyes full of excitement and lust.

> CELIA
> Let me read it.

RAFFI is uncomfortable. CELIA laughs.

                    CELIA (CONT'D)
         I'm sorry I'm making it hard to be
         the perfect son.

                    RAFFI
         I don't see why it has to be this
         way.

                    CELIA
         Yes you do.

CELIA takes RAFFI's hand and moves it down.

                    RAFFI
         I was happier when...you got along.

                    CELIA
         It wasn't as much fun.

                    RAFFI
         Says who?

CELIA pushes RAFFI to the floor, unbuttoning her shirt.

                    CELIA
         The ghost of the Father. My father.
         Not yours. Yours died like a hero.
         Mine died in a stupid accident.
         According to her.
              (beat)
         You look after your ghost, Raffi,
         and I'll look after mine.

                                        CUT TO:

12   EXT. VAN. TURKEY. COUNTRY. 1915 -- DAY

An Armenian sharpshooter locates a Turkish soldier, and fires
a bullet from an ancient rifle. Immediately, an Armenian
boy is commanded to retrieve the dead Turk's modern gun. As
bullets fly around him, the boy heroically retrieves the
gun, and hands it to an unarmed Armenian, who grabs it and
rushes to his position.

The Armenians are massively outnumbered by the huge Turkish
positions in the background. As the besieged Armenian rushes
to his position, a Turkish artillery shell explodes beside
him, throwing him forward. He is grabbed by two of his
comrades, who carry him away.

                                        CUT TO:

12A   INT. STUDIO. MISSION SET -- DAY

The Armenian soldiers bring their wounded comrade into the
courtyard of the American mission in Van. They are met by
an Armenian doctor. In the middle of this courtyard full of
women and children, MARTIN, playing Dr. Clarence Ussher,
addresses a group of young boys.

                    MARTIN
          To make sure that we get help, I am
          sending each of you out to deliver a
          copy of this letter...

Beside MARTIN, another actor in period costume translates
this into Armenian.

                  MARTIN (CONT'D)
          "To Americans, or any Foreign Consul.
          Internal troubles in Van. Turkey
          threatens to bombard American
          premises. Inform American Government
          that American lives are in danger...

The camera continues to widen out, revealing the film crew
shooting this scene. EDWARD is not happy.

                  EDWARD
    Cut.

The assistant director calls cut over his bullhorn, as EDWARD
takes MARTIN aside.

                  EDWARD (CONT'D)
          Martin, you are a great believer in
          Christ. You can't let these boys
          see your fear...

ROUBEN approaches the director and his star, not able to
contain himself.

                  ROUBEN
          You're a _missionary_. Think of what
          that means. This is a mission.
          You've traveled all the way from
          America to be with these people, to
          give them hope and assistance. Now
          these Christians are being wiped
          out. The city is surrounded by
          soldiers who will rape the women,
          butcher the men, and march the
          children to their deaths. You've
          got to be frightened. Absolutely
          terrified. Where is Christ?
                  (MORE)

                         ROUBEN (CONT'D)
          Why is this happening? Why doesn't
          anyone care?

Pause. ROUBEN suddenly realizes that he's crossed the line.
MARTIN stares at him with cool fury.

                         MARTIN
                    (with lethal precision)
          Be a pal, scamper over to craft
          service, and get me some water.
          Room temperature.

ROUBEN wilts. EDWARD gently pushes him aside, focusing his
energy on MARTIN.

                         EDWARD
                    (with patience and
                     calm)
          Let's try again.

                                                    CUT TO:

13   INT. ANI'S HOUSE. RAFFI'S ROOM -- MORNING

It's still very early. ANI enters her son's bedroom, opens
the shutters, and sits beside him.

                         ANI
          Did you give her my book?

RAFFI is awake.

                         RAFFI
          No...

                         ANI
          I told you not to. Is that why she
          came to my class?

                         RAFFI
          It's coming out next week. What's
          the difference?

                         ANI
          Is she coming to my talk? At the
          gallery?

                         RAFFI
          I...I'm not sure...

ANI gets up, clearly agitated by this news.

                    RAFFI (CONT'D)
          Maybe she'd ease off a bit if you
          didn't get so...defensive.

                    ANI
          Defensive? After what she's accused
          me of?

                    RAFFI
          This is all too weird for me...

                    ANI
          Smoking pot? Or sleeping with your
          step-sister?

Pause. Mother and son stare at each other.

                    RAFFI
          I'm old enough to...

                    ANI
          What are you trying to do, Raffi?
          Tell me this is normal? That she
          can continue to harass me? Tell
          people I'm somehow responsible for
          her father's death?

RAFFI doesn't respond.

                    ANI (CONT'D)
          No one asked her to move here. She
          could have stayed in Montreal.

                    RAFFI
          She needed us.

                    ANI
          What she needs is to destroy me the
          same way she thinks I destroyed him.

RAFFI's heard this before.

                    RAFFI
          Mom...

                    ANI
          She'll never understand the reasons
          why I stopped loving her father...

                    RAFFI
          Or for seeing someone else.

                    ANI
          I'm not accountable to her.

                              RAFFI
                    I am.

                              ANI
                    Why?

                              RAFFI
                    Because I love her.

ANI looks at RAFFI, not wanting to believe this.

                                        CUT TO:

14   INT. ALI'S APARTMENT.   LIVING/DINING AREA -- DAY

      PHILIP, ALI, DAVID and TONY are seated around a dinner table.

                              DAVID
                    Tony, would you like to say grace?

ALI and PHILIP eye each other, as TONY nods and bows his
head.

                              TONY
                    For what we are about to receive may
                    the Lord make us truly grateful.

                              DAVID
                    Amen.

The three men begin their dinner.   TONY looks up at his
father.

                              TONY
                    Dad?

                              PHILIP
                    Yes?

                              TONY
                    Why don't you say 'amen'?

PHILIP looks at DAVID, then back at his son.

                              PHILIP
                    I say it inside.

                              TONY
                    Inside where?

                              PHILIP
                    Inside my head.

                         TONY
            Can God hear it inside your head?

                        PHILIP
            What do you think, Dad?

DAVID remains silent, not wanting to get into this argument.
ALI tries to break the tension.

                         ALI
            God can hear all your thoughts.
            Even if you're wearing a really thick
            hat.

                        TONY
            But you don't believe in God.

ALI is surprised by this response. He looks at DAVID, who
continues eating.

                                              CUT TO:

15   EXT. JANET'S HOUSE -- DAY

PHILIP watches DAVID leave TONY with his mother, then walk
back to his car. DAVID sits down beside his son, heavy with
the conversation he knows he will have.

                        PHILIP
            Here's the situation, Dad. Whenever
            Tony comes over alone, he's fine.
            We play, he laughs, he's full of
            joy. Whenever you're around, he
            becomes quiet and withdrawn...and we
            can't stand it.

                        DAVID
            That's not true, Philip.

                        PHILIP
            The more oppression you...

                        DAVID
            Oppression! He loves when I'm there.

                        PHILIP
            ...the more you bring this heavy
            cloud into our apartment, the more
            he believes that the way we live is
            wrong.

                        DAVID
            I've never told him that.

                        PHILIP
          You don't need to. He can feel your
          disgust...

                        DAVID
          Philip...

                        PHILIP
          And where did he pick up that Ali
          doesn't believe in God?

                        DAVID
          He asked me why your friend didn't
          say grace with us...

                        PHILIP
          My 'friend'...

                        DAVID
          I said he had his own God. It's
          true, isn't it?

PHILIP looks at DAVID, darkly.

                        DAVID (CONT'D)
          Philip, I'm trying very hard to accept
          this all. I really am.
               (beat)
          And I don't believe that he's
          miserable when I'm around. In fact...

                        PHILIP
          Dad, you're retiring soon. You're
          going to have alot of time on your
          hands. Either you make an effort to
          change your attitude, or you're not
          welcome at our place anymore.

                        DAVID
               (beat, he considers)
          And I just see him with Janet?

                        PHILIP
          Janet has her own parents to deal
          with.

                                              CUT TO:

16   INT. ARSHILE GORKY'S STUDIO. NEW YORK CITY. 1935 -- DAY

GORKY has finished the gridded sketch of his mother and him.
He has attached it on the wall of his studio, right beside
the photograph that is its inspiration.

On an easel, GORKY has begun the oil painting that will become
his masterpiece. He looks to the photograph for inspiration,
then to the sketch for technical direction.

>   ANI
>   (voice over)
>   The only surviving photograph of
>   young Gorky was taken in Van in 1912.
>   It was intended to be sent to his
>   father, who had left for America
>   years before. As we look at the
>   eyes of Gorky and his mother, we can
>   imagine them wondering why he had
>   left them alone...

DETAIL on the two faces in the photograph, then ARSHILE GORKY
looking at the portrait.

>   CUT TO:

17   EXT. VAN. TURKEY. COUNTRY. 1912 -- DAY

YOUNG GORKY and his mother, SHUSHAN, walk towards the walled
city which is perched dramatically on a large rock.

>   ANI
>   (voice over continuing)
>   ...it was a beautiful, sunny day as
>   Shushan took Gorky to the old city
>   of Van. The serrated medieval wall
>   of the citadel cast a broad silhouette
>   against the brilliant sky...

>   CUT TO:

18   EXT. VAN. TURKEY. STREET. 1912 -- DAY

SHUSHAN and YOUNG GORKY walk down a crowded street towards
the front of a photographer's studio.

>   ANI
>   (voice over continuing)
>   ...That day Gorky wore a long formal
>   overcoat with a felt collar. He had
>   dark trousers, and classical Armenian
>   slipper shoes. Shushan's dress was
>   covered, except for the arms, by a
>   long flowered apron...

>   CUT TO:

18A   EXT. VAN. TURKEY. STREET. PHOTORAPHER'S AREA. 1912 -- DAY

A PHOTOGRAPHER has set up an outdoor 'studio' with a backdrop
against a wall. SHUSHAN and YOUNG GORKY position themselves
in front of this backdrop, readying themselves for their
portrait.

SEVAN, a boy slightly younger than YOUNG GORKY, is the
PHOTOGRAPHER's assistant.

                                                CUT TO:

19   INT. ART GALLERY. COURT -- NIGHT

ANI is giving a lecture to a group of people in the atrium.
Behind her, a slide of the famous photograph is projected.

                    ANI
              This was a convention of all studio
              photographers. The flowers were
              offered as a fragrant gift to the
              recipient...

ANGLE ON

CELIA and RAFFI, seated together, listening to ANI's lecture.
RAFFI can sense that CELIA is up to something. She raises
her hand.

ANI notices CELIA's raised hand. She takes a moment, then
responds.

                    ANI (CONT'D)
              Yes?

                    CELIA
              I'm confused. Had Gorky changed his
              name by this point?

                    ANI
              No. He changed it in his twenties.
              After he arrived in the United States.

                    CELIA
              So why aren't you calling him by his
              real name? Vosdanig Adoian.

                    ANI
              I could. If it would make things
              clearer.

CELIA looks at the audience. RAFFI crouches in his chair,
embarrassed by CELIA's tactic.

                              CELIA
                    Am I the only person confused by
                    this? It seems to me that when a
                    man who's so proud of where he's
                    from changes his name, we have to
                    wonder why. Why would he deny his
                    identity?

ANI waits a beat, then continues her lecture while CELIA
remains standing, waiting for a response. Behind CELIA,
EDWARD, the film director, is also trying to listen to ANI's
lecture. He is upset by CELIA's interruption.

                              ANI
                        (back to her lecture)
                    Gorky looks prematurely solemn, with
                    almond eyes in an oval face, his
                    hair combed neatly to the side.
                    Shushan looks bravely at the camera,
                    challenging her absent husband with
                    the trials of her life...

                              CELIA
                        (still standing,
                         defiant)
                    Why would you say that?

ANI stops and stares at CELIA.

                              CELIA (CONT'D)
                    Isn't it obvious he knew the Armenians
                    were about to be massacred? He went
                    to America to prepare a life for his
                    family. They wanted to send him a
                    photograph to let him know they're
                    still alive. There's nothing
                    challenging about it.

                              ANI
                        (slight pause)
                    Gorky never understood why his father
                    didn't return...

                              CELIA
                    Because he would have been killed.

                              ANI
                    So he left his family to die alone?

ANI immediately regrets her emotional response. Pause.

                              RAFFI
                        (under his breath)
                    Celia...

                    CELIA
          Aren't you confusing Gorky's father
          with your dead husband? I mean,
          your first dead husband. The one
          who was shot by police.

ANGLE ON

PHILIP, who works as a security guard at the gallery.

                    CELIA (CONT'D)
          The terrorist. You said, at the
          time, that by trying to murder a
          Turkish diplomat fifteen years ago
          he was betraying you. You felt
          abandoned.

EDWARD, blocked by CELIA, can't stand this anymore.

                    EDWARD
          Excuse me.

CELIA ignores EDWARD, continuing to stare at ANI.

                    CELIA
          This is all about you.

                    EDWARD
          Miss. We are here to listen to this
          lecture. Now please...

The audience begins to applaud. CELIA is defeated. She
looks to RAFFI, who seems frozen with indecision and fear.
CELIA speaks under her breath to RAFFI.

                    CELIA
          Let's go.

CELIA begins to leave. RAFFI remains frozen. ANI switches
the slide to the painting of Gorky's masterpiece, "The Artist
and His Mother'.

                    ANI
          The Artist and His Mother is not
          simply a painted version of a
          photograph. The differences underline
          the expressive elements that make
          this such a powerful work of art...

ANI stares at her son as he remains rooted to his chair.

ANI (CONT'D)
Gorky's homage to his mother was
bound to take on a sacred quality.
His experience as a survivor of the
Armenian Genocide is at the root of
its spiritual power. With this
painting, Gorky had saved his mother
from oblivion, snatching her out of
a pile of corpses to place her on a
pedestal.

RAFFI, staring at his mother, slowly gets up and begins to
walk out of the hall to join CELIA. ANI seems heartbroken.

CUT TO:

20   INT. ARSHILE GORKY'S STUDIO. NEW YORK CITY. 1935 -- DAY

Details from the photograph, the sketch, and the painting
that GORKY is working on.

ANGLE ON

GORKY's face as he brushes paint onto the canvas. He begins
to sing a song to himself.

CUT TO:

21   EXT. VAN. TURKEY. STREET. PHOTORAPHER'S AREA. 1912 -- DAY

Over GORKY's song, the image of YOUNG GORKY posing for the
famous photograph. Beside the PHOTOGRAPHER, his young son,
SEVAN, holds a reflector board, reflecting soft sunlight
onto YOUNG GORKY's face.

The two boys smile at each other. The seeds of a friendship.

SEVAN puts the reflector board down for a moment, and moves
to pluck a white orchid from the ground. He brings this to
YOUNG GORKY, to hold in his hand. SEVAN moves back to his
position with the reflector board as the historic photograph
is taken.

CUT TO:

22   INT. WAREHOUSE -- NIGHT

CELIA and RAFFI are making love. CELIA senses that RAFFI's
mind is elsewhere.

CELIA
What is it?

                         RAFFI
          Why did you bring up my Dad?

                         CELIA
          It's true, isn't it?

                         RAFFI
          He didn't run away. My mother had
          to distance herself from him...

                         CELIA
               (ironic)
          To save the family.

                         RAFFI
          He wasn't a terrorist.

                         CELIA
          I didn't say he was.

                         RAFFI
          You said he was a terrorist.

                         CELIA
          Did I?

                         RAFFI
          Yeah.

                         CELIA
          Well, I suppose you could see it
          that way. I mean, he was about to
          assassinate a diplomat...

                         RAFFI
          He was a freedom fighter. There's a
          difference.

                         CELIA
          Sure. It was a really cool way to
          go. A lot better than my Dad, jumping
          off a cliff.

Pause.

                         RAFFI
          Jumping?

                         CELIA
          He committed suicide.

                         RAFFI
          That's new. Wasn't the story that
          my mother pushed him off the cliff?

CELIA pulls herself away from her lovemaking position with
RAFFI.

>   CELIA
>   The story? You think I'm making up
>   a story?

>   RAFFI
>   No, I meant...

>   CELIA
>   (disgusted)
>   This is no way to fuck.

>   CUT TO:

23   INT. ART GALLERY. COURT -- NIGHT

At a small reception after the lecture, ANI has been
approached by EDWARD and ROUBEN, the screenwriter. ANI stares
at EDWARD, stunned by his presence.

>   ANI
>   I'm sorry, I'm just so shocked to
>   see you here. I've seen all your
>   films, and...

ANI is speechless. EDWARD makes a reassuring gesture.

>   EDWARD
>   Please...

>   ROUBEN
>   We're the ones that are shocked.
>   I've been working on this screenplay
>   for five years, done as much research
>   as possible, and then you come up
>   with this.

>   ANI
>   With what?

>   ROUBEN
>   That Arshile Gorky was a child during
>   the rebellion in Van. That he was
>   there.

ANI looks at EDWARD.

>   EDWARD
>   My mother was a genocide survivor.
>   All my life I promised to make a
>   film that would tell her story.
>   (MORE)

                    EDWARD (CONT'D)
          How she suffered. Now, we are making
          that film.

                    ROUBEN
          We had a day off, and decided to
          check out the art gallery. We noticed
          that you were giving this talk...

                    ANI
          I'm not understanding something. Is
          Gorky in your film?

                    EDWARD
          Not yet.

                    ROUBEN
          As you were speaking, we got very
          excited about the idea of working
          him in. As another character...well,
          not an entirely new character, but a
          character we can build on.

                    ANI
          How?

                    ROUBEN
          There's a young boy in the film...

                    EDWARD
          He will be Gorky.

                    ANI
          You'll change the script?

                    ROUBEN
          Not really. Just add to what's there.
          It's a minor character we can develop.
          Thread that layer through the story.
          This amazing artist, as a kid,
          remembering what happened to him.
          See what I mean?
               (beat)
          It'd be great to have you as a
          consultant.

EDWARD looks at ANI with great sincerity and feeling.

                    EDWARD
          You have offered us a gift.
               (MORE)

                    EDWARD (CONT'D)
          From the ashes of all that has been
          destroyed, we can open this gift
          together.

                                              CUT TO:

24   INT. TORONTO AIRPORT. CUSTOMS STATION -- NIGHT

      RAFFI has been routed for a customs inspection. He is
      carrying a large duffel bag. He has placed it on a counter.
      DAVID is busy punching something into a computer terminal.
      After a moment, he looks up at RAFFI, ready to begin the
      inspection.

      RAFFI looks different. He is unshaven, and appears older.
      He has come back from a long journey.

                    DAVID
          Where are you coming from?

                    RAFFI
          Turkey.

                    DAVID
          Direct?

                    RAFFI
          Yes.

      DAVID looks at the duffel bag.

                    DAVID
          Can I open this?

                    RAFFI
          Sure.

      DAVID unzips the bag to reveal sealed cans of film.

                    DAVID
          What are these?

                    RAFFI
          Film. Motion picture film. Here...

      RAFFI hands DAVID a piece of paper. DAVID glances over it.

                    DAVID
          This sort of thing is usually done
          through a bonder.

                    RAFFI
          They wanted me to hand deliver it.

                    DAVID
          'They'?

                    RAFFI
          The director. It's very valuable
          footage.

DAVID picks up one of the canisters.

                    DAVID
          Can you open this?

                    RAFFI
          No...

DAVID stares at RAFFI.

                    RAFFI (CONT'D)
          ...it's exposed film. It would
          destroy it.

DAVID continues to stare at RAFFI, a slight smile on his
lips.

                    DAVID
          Oh.

                    RAFFI
          It's for a movie that's being shot
          here. In Canada. We had to go to
          Turkey to get some process shots.

                    DAVID
          What sort of process?

                    RAFFI
          Shots that will be used for digital
          effects. Plates.

                    DAVID
          I don't understand.

                    RAFFI
          We needed scenes of hundreds of people
          passing through these places. Instead
          of taking actors and extras to the
          middle of nowhere, it's cheaper to
          shoot empty shots of locations, then
          add the people in later on.

DAVID stares hard at RAFFI. Another Customs Officer
approaches DAVID and says something to him. DAVID nods,
then looks back to RAFFI.

                         DAVID
          Excuse me for a moment.

DAVID leaves with the other GUARD. RAFFI is alone.

                                        CUT TO:

25   INT. STUDIO. MISSION SET -- DAY

EDWARD is walking ANI through the studio set of the American
Mission in Van.

                         EDWARD
          Much of this is based on descriptions
          that my mother told me.

ANI stops dead in her tracks. On one of the painted
backdrops, she sees an image of Mount Ararat.

                         EDWARD (CONT'D)
          What is it?

                         ANI
          You wouldn't be able to see Mount
          Ararat from Van.

                         EDWARD
              (slightly embarrassed)
          Well...yes. I felt it would be
          important.

                         ANI
          But it's not true.

                         EDWARD
          It's true in spirit.

ROUBEN joins ANI and EDWARD. He is carrying a copy of ANI's
book.

                         ROUBEN
          Sorry, I had a call...

                         EDWARD
          Did we get our Turk?

                         ROUBEN
          We put the offer into his agent.

                         EDWARD
          Rouben, Ani is confused about the
          mountain.

                    ROUBEN
          Ararat?

                    EDWARD
          She has noticed, quite correctly,
          that it would not be seen from Van.

                    ROUBEN
          Well, we thought we could stretch
          things a bit. It's such an
          identifiable symbol, and given the
          moment in history we're trying to
          show...

                    ANI
          It's something you could justify.

                    ROUBEN
          Sure. Poetic license.

                    ANI
          Where do you get those?

                    ROUBEN
          What?

                    ANI
          Poetic licenses?

                    ROUBEN
          Wherever you can.

Pause. ROUBEN stares at ANI, slightly on edge.

                    ANI
             (smiling)
          So that's my job? To let you feel
          better about distorting things?

                    EDWARD
          The young boy in our film gets sent
          by Ussher to deliver a letter. He
          gets caught by the Turks...

ANI is confused.

                    ROUBEN
          That's the character we'd make into
          Gorky.

                    ANI
          How?

                         ROUBEN
          Well, using my poetic license, I can
          build up the story around him...with
          your help. Scenes with his mother,
          maybe something where he sees his
          best friend get...I don't
          know...tortured to death...

                         ANI
          But we don't know if that happened.

                         ROUBEN
          And we never will.

A moment. ANI absorbs this.

                         ANI
          So how does he get caught?

                         ROUBEN
          By April of 1915 the Turks had
          surrounded the Armenian Quarter.
          Within the quarter, inside these
          fortified walls, is the American
          mission, run by a doctor, Clarence
          Ussher...

As ROUBEN explains the scene cuts to...

                                                    CUT TO:

25A   EXT. VAN. TURKEY. COUNTRY. 1915 -- DAY

The camera glides past Armenian soldiers defending their
position...

                         ROUBEN (V.O.)
          Outside a few hundred men with ancient
          guns are surrounded by well-armed
          troops with the latest in European
          artillery. Miraculously, through
          their ingenuity and teamwork these
          men and women are able to hold the
          Armenian position. But they're
          completely isolated, cut from all
          contact with the outside world.
          Ussher has to let the Americans know
          what is about to happen. He hopes
          one of these boys will get through...

The camera focuses on two young boys making their way through
the shells and smoke.

They are identified as YOUNG GORKY and his friend, SEVAN.

                                                    CUT TO:

26   INT. ART GALLERY. MASTERS GALLERY -- DAY

PHILIP is wandering through a brightly lit gallery, where he
works as a security guard. He comes upon a group of school
children sitting in front of an art education TEACHER,
explaining a painting to the kids. PHILIP smiles warmly at
the attentive kids as ALI approaches him from behind. ALI
plants a kiss on his neck. PHILIP, surprised, swings around,
making sure no one sees this.

                    PHILIP
          How did it go?

                    ALI
               (excited)
          I think I was great.

                    PHILIP
          They liked you?

                    ALI
          I think so.

                    PHILIP
          When do you find out?

                    ALI
          They said they'd let me know...

ALI's cell phone rings. ALI and PHILIP share a suspended
moment of mutual anticipation.

                    ALI (CONT'D)
          Hello?

ALI lets out a yelp of joy, and throws his arms around PHILIP,
who is embarrassed by this situation, but wanting to share
ALI's good news. The school children all turn around to see
what's going on.

The art teacher raises her eyebrows with good-natured
inquisitiveness.

                    ART TEACHER
          Good news?

                    PHILIP
          He just got a big part. In a movie.

PHILIP nods as ALI finishes up with his agent on the phone.

                         CHILD
          Does he play a good guy or a bad
          guy?

ALI approaches the CHILD with playful menace, growling like
a vicious monster.

                          ALI
          I play a very...<u>very</u>...Bad guy.

The school children all squeal in scared delight at ALI.

                                              CUT TO:

27   INT. STUDIO. JEVDET BEY'S BUREAU. VAN. TURKEY. 1912 -- DAY

JEVDET BEY, the Turkish governor of Van, inspects a portrait
of him that has been taken by the PHOTOGRAPHER. The
PHOTOGRAPHER waits nervously for JEVDET BEY's response.
SEVAN, the PHOTOGRAPHER's son stands waiting beside his
father.

JEVDET BEY is played by ALI. He nods in approval.

                     ALI AS JEVDET BEY
          Very good.

The PHOTOGRAPHER cautiously speaks up, as his young son,
SEVAN, watches nervously.

                     PHOTOGRAPHER
          Effendi?

                     ALI AS JEVDET BEY
          Yes?

                     PHOTOGRAPHER
          Can we discuss a payment?

Immediate tension. SEVAN moves beside his father, who places
his hand comfortingly on the young boy's shoulder. JEVDET
BEY moves towards the PHOTOGRAPHER, taking his portfolio
from him. He places the portfolio on his desk, flipping
through a series of family portraits that the PHOTOGRAPHER
has taken.

                     ALI AS JEVDET BEY
          Do you know what I think of as I
          look at these faces?

                     PHOTOGRAPHER
          No, Effendi.

                    ALI AS JEVDET BEY
          I think of what's in their mind as
          they stare at your camera. Their
          desperate need to be remembered.
          'For what?' , we may ask. Are they
          particularly brilliant men, wonderful
          mothers, respectful and promising
          children? In reality, no matter how
          beautifully you photograph them -
          whatever moment you may capture with
          your lens - it's a lie. They are
          doomed to be forgotten.

JEVDET BEY hands the portfolio back to the PHOTOGRAPHER.

                    JEVDET BEY
          A payment is a gesture of thanks,
          no?

                    PHOTOGRAPHER
          Yes, Effendi.

                    ALI AS JEVDET BEY
          So let us examine what it is you
          have to be thankful for. A man of
          my position has chosen you to take
          his portrait. This has brought you
          prestige and honor. How will you
          give thanks?

ALI extends his hand to the PHOTOGRAPHER. After a brief
pause, the PHOTOGRAPHER takes his hand and kisses it.

                    JEVDET BEY
          You're welcome.

ALI as JEVDET BEY moves his hand to SEVAN.

                    JEVDET BEY (CONT'D)
          Would you like to thank me as well?

SEVAN can't respond. JEVDET BEY extracts a pocket watch
from SEVAN's jacket, staring at it in his hand.

                    PHOTOGRAPHER
          Sevan...?

The boy is frozen in fear. JEVDET BEY puts the pocket watch
back.

                    JEVDET BEY
          We shall find another time. Another
          means. There are different ways to
          express gratitude.

JEVDET BEY smiles at the defiant young boy.

                                        CUT TO:

28   INT. ANI'S HOUSE.   KITCHEN -- MORNING

ANI watches her son as he eats his breakfast. He is consumed
with the food on his plate and rarely makes eye contact with
her.

                    RAFFI
          So do it.

                    ANI
          That's it? That's all you have to
          say? Edward Saroyan is one of the
          greatest directors in the world.

                    RAFFI
          Are they paying you?

                    ANI
          Yes.

                    RAFFI
               (concentrating on his
                 food)
          Great.

                    ANI
          Raffi, you know how long I've been
          working on this. If it can help
          Gorky's story get told...

                    RAFFI
               (bland)
          Go for it.

ANI stares at RAFFI.

                    RAFFI (CONT'D)
          What?

                    ANI
          Why do you still sleep here?

                    RAFFI
          It's my home.

                    ANI
          Doesn't she want you there?

                    RAFFI
          It's uncomfortable. Too humid.

Pause. RAFFI gets up to get some more cereal.

                    ANI
          Can we talk about what happened the
          other night?

                    RAFFI
          Sure...

                    ANI
          That's why she wanted to read the
          book. So she could humiliate me.

                    RAFFI
          So? Fight back.

                    ANI
          Don't be ridiculous. She knows next
          to nothing about art, and I'm
          certainly not going to answer her
          accusations.

                    RAFFI
          You seemed to be doing a pretty good
          job.

                    ANI
          What are you talking about?

                    RAFFI
          The way you use history like a weapon.
          Talking about Gorky's mother as a
          way of...attacking Celia's issues.

                    ANI
          Celia's 'issues'? Are you out of
          your mind? It was a prepared lecture.

RAFFI can't respond.

                    ANI (CONT'D)
          Celia believes I murdered her father.
          That I pushed him off a cliff. Would
          I do this? Would you like to believe
          that your mother's a killer? Is
          this remotely possible to you?

                    RAFFI
               (after a beat)
          Her new theory is that you made him
          jump.

                    ANI
          How?

                    RAFFI
          Something you said. She thinks the
          whole last chapter of the book is a
          way of admitting guilt.

                    ANI
               (mockingly)
          Oh, I see. The idea being that since
          Gorky committed suicide, her father
          must have as well. Is that what she
          does all day?
               (beat)
          Lie around getting high and dreaming
          up paranoid fantasies?

                    RAFFI
          It's easy to make fun of her.

                    ANI
          Not as easy as you think.

RAFFI starts to leave.

                    ANI (CONT'D)
          I can get you a job on the film.
          Would you be interested?

                    RAFFI
          Doing what?

                    ANI
          They need a driver.

                    RAFFI
          Would I get to hang around the set?
          Watch the 'great man' at work?

                    ANI
          I can ask.

                    RAFFI
          Okay. Might be fun.

ANI stares at her son.

                    ANI
          Raffi, she wants her father's death
          to be more meaningful than it was.
          It gives her a cause.

                    RAFFI
          And we all know how dangerous those
          can be.

                    ANI
          She has no right to compare the two
          men. Your father died for something
          he believed in.

                    RAFFI
          I just wish I had some idea what
          that was.

RAFFI stares at his mother.

                                        CUT TO:

29   EXT. NORTHERN QUEBEC -- DAY

CELIA and RAFFI are walking through a forest. They approach
a rocky cliff.

RAFFI stops. CELIA walks towards the edge of the cliff.

                    RAFFI
          Celia...

                    CELIA
          I know. Be careful. That's what my
          father used to tell me. He was a
          cautious man. He never came closer
          to the edge than where you're standing
          right now.

CELIA turns around. She has her back to the edge. She takes
a step backward.

                    RAFFI
               (terrified)
          Celia...

                    CELIA
          But accidents happen. According to
          your mother. People fall. Just
          like that.

                    RAFFI
          Please, let's go.

                    CELIA
          Do you think she's responsible?

                    RAFFI
          For what?

CELIA takes another step back. She has to balance herself
from falling.

                    CELIA
          Do you?

                    RAFFI
          What are you talking about?

                    CELIA
          I'm talking about the way my father
          died.

                    RAFFI
          Celia...

                    CELIA
          Raffi, I wish this wasn't an issue
          for me. I'm smart enough to know
          that it's bad to carry these things;
          that they eat away at you.

                    RAFFI
          Something terrible happened here.
          Something that has hurt you...

                    CELIA
          Why do you care?

                    RAFFI
          Because I love you.

RAFFI slowly moves forward. He takes CELIA into his arms,
and embraces her. He pulls her back from the edge.

CELIA turns him around.

                    CELIA
          Prove it. Close your eyes.

RAFFI stares at CELIA.

                    CELIA (CONT'D)
          Close them.

He does. She gently takes him one step closer to the edge.

                    CELIA (CONT'D)
          Keep them closed.

                    RAFFI
          What are you doing?

                    CELIA
          Do you trust me?

She comes closer and repeats more softly in his ear. She directs him to the edge of the cliff.

                    CELIA (CONT'D)
          Do you trust me?

                    RAFFI
          Yes...

He opens his eyes and stares deeply into hers.

                                             CUT TO:

30   INT. TORONTO AIRPORT. CUSTOMS STATION -- NIGHT

DAVID comes back from his meeting with the other Customs Officer. He is looking at the piece of paper that RAFFI had given him.

                    DAVID
          This film was shot in Toronto almost
          a year ago.

                    RAFFI
          That's right.

                    DAVID
          And now you're coming back from Turkey
          with these cans of footage.

RAFFI gives DAVID another piece of paper. RAFFI appears nervous as DAVID reads the document.

                    DAVID (CONT'D)
          This tells me that you worked on
          this film as a production assistant
          and driver. This is a letter of
          recommendation for future employment.
          It does not explain why you are
          returning from Turkey months later.

RAFFI takes a moment to respond.

                    RAFFI
          There was some stuff they needed
          from Turkey. We...added a character.

                    DAVID
          Who's 'we'?

                    RAFFI
          The director and the writer...and my
          mother...

                    DAVID
          Your mother?

                    RAFFI
          Yes. She's an art history professor.

                    DAVID
              (beat)
          Who is this new character?

                    RAFFI
          Arshile Gorky.

                    DAVID
          A Turkish painter?

                    RAFFI

          Armenian.

                    DAVID
          Why would you go to Turkey to shoot
          an Armenian painter?

                    RAFFI
          Because that's where he was from.
          He was born there. Armenia was
          historically...Eastern Turkey.
          Anatolia...

This history is too murky for DAVID. He continues.

                    DAVID
          So you went back to Turkey to shoot
          some stuff with Arshile Gorky?

                    RAFFI
          No...I mean...Arshile Gorky is dead.
          It was some stuff that took place
          where he was born.

                    DAVID
          And they sent you there alone?
          Without a crew?

                    RAFFI
          Yes. They couldn't get permission
          to send a crew there.

                    DAVID
          Why not?

                         RAFFI
          It's not easy to shoot a story about
          the Armenian genocide in Turkey.
          It's politically...sensitive.

                         DAVID
          In what way?

                         RAFFI
          Because the Turkish authorities don't
          want to admit it happened.

                         DAVID
          Why not?

                         RAFFI
               (beat, slight smile)
          You'd have to ask them.

DAVID looks into RAFFI's eyes, weighing what he has heard.

                         DAVID
          So what's this story about?

RAFFI is unsure where to begin.

                                               CUT TO:

31   EXT. STUDIO. MISSION SET -- DAY

In the crowded courtyard of the American Mission in Van.
MARTIN, playing USSHER, is finishing a prayer to the group
of young boys.

                    MARTIN AS USSHER
          ...But deliver us from evil, For
          thine is The Kingdom, The Power and
          The Glory, for ever and ever. Amen...

The camera moves onto the face of YOUNG GORKY who holds one
of the letters in his hand. SEVAN, his young friend, stands
beside him.

                    MARTIN AS USSHER (CONT'D)
          Godspeed to you all...

YOUNG GORKY stares at the letter that has been given to him
to deliver. He begins to walk through the crowd to find his
mother. SEVAN follows him.

The following conversation is in Armenian.

                    YOUNG GORKY
          We have to go.

                         SHUSHAN
              God bless you.

SHUSHAN kisses her beloved son. She hands him a picture,
taken from the portrait studio three years ago. It is the
famous portrait upon which GORKY will base his masterpiece.

                         SHUSHAN (CONT'D)
              Do you remember when we took this
              picture to send to your father?

                         YOUNG GORKY
              Yes.

                         SHUSHAN
              If the Turks capture you, you will
              never give up your faith. You will
              never forget your mother tongue. If
              you survive, it will be to tell this
              story. Of what has happened here.
              Of what will happen...

                         YOUNG GORKY
              We will win, Mother.

                         SHUSHAN
              Take this picture with you. You
              will not forget me.

                         YOUNG GORKY
              We will win.

                         SHUSHAN
              As God wills.

SHUSHAN embraces her son as SEVAN watches.

                                                 CUT TO:

32   EXT. VAN. TURKEY. STREET. 1915 -- DAY

YOUNG GORKY and SEVAN running through the besieged streets
of Van. They run past the bodies of people massacred in the
street. Houses are burning. Turkish soldiers are pulling
valuables from looted stores.

Suddenly, the two boys realize that they are being chased by
a soldier on horseback.

                                                 CUT TO:

33   INT. STUDIO. JEVDET BEY'S BUREAU. VAN. 1915 -- DAY

ALI is playing JEVDET BEY, instructing a soldier on the finer
points of his favorite means of torture. He selects a small
horseshoe from a tray of horseshoes presented to him.

Behind him, SEVAN is held by a large soldier. SEVAN is bare
foot.

                    JEVDET BEY
          I want you to remember that this has
          to be nailed into the ball of the
          heel. Not the sole.

JEVDET BEY places the horseshoe onto SEVAN's bare foot.

                    JEVDET BEY (CONT'D)
          There's no bone in the sole. It'll
          fall off. Alright?

The soldier nods and disappears from the office with the
captive SEVAN.

From a adjoining room, SEVAN's screams are heard as this
horrific torture is administered on the young boy off screen.

JEVDET BEY settles into his chair to read the letter from
USSHER that has been found. The terrified YOUNG GORKY is
seated in front of him.

                    ALI AS JEVDET BEY
          An appeal for Christian help. Does
          your missionary think we are such
          monsters? If we had such a hatred
          for you Christians, would we have
          allowed you to keep your churches?
          We have invested the Greeks and
          Armenians with power and freedom.
          You should be thankful.

ALI, playing JEVDET BEY, looks at the photograph of GORKY
and SHUSHAN which has been confiscated from the young boy.

                    ALI AS JEVDET BEY (CONT'D)
          Is this your mother?

YOUNG GORKY nods.

                    ALI AS JEVDET BEY (CONT'D)
          She's very beautiful. Is she inside
          the mission now?

YOUNG GORKY nods.

                    ALI AS JEVDET BEY (CONT'D)
          She has given you this photograph so
          that you may remember her. Look at
          it now.

YOUNG GORKY stares at the photograph that JEVDET BEY holds
out at him.

                    ALI AS JEVDET BEY (CONT'D)
          This is the face of a woman who has
          raised you to feel superior to us.
          She has taught you that Turks are
          vengeful and ignorant. That we are
          bloodthirsty.

JEVDET BEY throws the photograph back at YOUNG GORKY.

                    ALI AS JEVDET BEY (CONT'D)
          Now I will teach you something.
          What is about to happen to your people
          is your own fault. As much as you
          talk about your prophet Jesus Christ,
          in the depths of your hearts you
          believe in nothing but money and
          commerce. My streets are overrun
          with your markets and moneylenders.
          Your greed has led us to corruption
          and ruin. And now, you yourselves
          will be ruined.

The camera pulls back to reveal EDWARD and his crew. RAFFI
is observing EDWARD's face as he shoots this emotional scene.

SEVAN's screams of pain continue in the background. Suddenly,
they come to a stop.

ALI, playing JEVDET BEY, hands a document to YOUNG GORKY.

                    ALI AS JEVDET BEY (CONT'D)
          Take this back to your American
          missionary. He must sign it, or
          allow us to bring fifty soldiers
          into the compound...

                                                      CUT TO:

34   INT. TORONTO AIRPORT. CUSTOMS STATION -- NIGHT

RAFFI is recounting this story to DAVID.

                    DAVID
          What did he want him to sign?

                      RAFFI
It was a document stating that Ussher
refused Turkish protection.

                      DAVID
But that's obvious. He was helping
to protect the Armenians with their
self-defence.

                      RAFFI
Exactly. Ussher and Jevdet Bey had
met a few times before. He tried to
stop him from carrying out his plans.

                      DAVID
What plans?

                      RAFFI
For genocide.
    (beat)
Over a million people were killed.
An ancient civilization living on
ancestral land...

                                       CUT TO:

35   EXT. VAN. TURKEY. 1915. STREET -- DAY

Hundreds of bodies are strewn along the side of the road.
Dogs fight with each other over the carcass of a child.

On a makeshift gallows, the bodies of men dangling; a mother
wails under the suspended body of her murdered son.

USSHER (played by MARTIN) is walking through this street in
Van, witnessing the carnage. Beside him, YOUNG GORKY carries
an American flag.

                                       CUT TO:

36   INT. STUDIO. JEVDET BEY'S BUREAU. VAN. 1915 -- DAY

On the studio set, EDWARD is directing the following scene
between USSHER (played by MARTIN) and JEVDET BEY (played by
ALI).

RAFFI is watching the mechanics of this scene very closely,
watching EDWARD like a hawk.

                  ALI AS JEVDET BEY
I need permission to put fifty
soldiers with canon and supplies in
your mission compound.

> MARTIN AS USSHER
> Why?

> ALI AS JEVDET BEY
> To protect you.

> MARTIN AS USSHER
> We are under the protection of the
> United States of America.

> ALI AS JEVDET BEY
> Yes. But America is so far away.

Pause.   USSHER stares hard at JEVDET BEY.

> MARTIN AS USSHER
> It won't be safe to send so many
> Turkish soldiers into the heart of
> the Armenian quarter. It's bound to
> cause trouble.
> (beat)
> What danger are you trying to protect
> us from?

JEVDET BEY doesn't respond.

> ALI AS JEVDET BEY
> (short pause)
> If you have a problem with taking my
> soldiers, then you must sign this
> statement that you have refused the
> protection of the Turkish government.

ANGLE ON

RAFFI watching the shooting of this scene as his voice is
heard explaining to DAVID...

> RAFFI
> (voice over)
> If Ussher signed this statement, it
> would be like giving the Turks
> permission to slaughter the Americans
> in the compound the same way they
> were massacring the Armenians outside.

CUT TO:

37   INT. TORONTO AIRPORT. CUSTOMS STATION -- NIGHT

> DAVID
> You've lost me.

                        RAFFI
          It was the same document he had
          presented to the boy. If the United
          States government ever made any
          inquiry into the incident, that
          statement - the document the Turks
          wanted Ussher to sign - would affirm
          that the Americans were offered
          protection, but that they refused.

                        DAVID
          And if he let them in...?

                        RAFFI
          The Turks would use it as a strategic
          point. With that many soldiers and
          artillery based in the mission, they'd
          have a foothold in the Armenian
          quarter.

                        DAVID
          A Trojan horse.

                        RAFFI
          Right.

                        DAVID
          So what did he do?

                                                    CUT TO:

38   INT. STUDIO. JEVDET BEY'S BUREAU. VAN. 1915 -- DAY

      As the camera rolls, MARTIN rises dramatically and raises
      the document in his hand. RAFFI is watching.

                        MARTIN AS USSHER
          Our premises are part of the United
          States of America. They are
          extraterritorial by treaty right,
          and completely neutral. We will
          preserve this neutrality to the last.

      MARTIN dramatically rips the document in half, and hands it
      back to JEVDET BEY.

                                                    CUT TO:

39   EXT. VAN. TURKEY. BARN. 1915 -- NIGHT

      YOUNG GORKY runs into a barn where a group of men and women
      are working on supplies and captured armaments. He finds
      the PHOTOGRAPHER, working on repairing a machine gun.

                    RAFFI (V.O.)
          There were only a few hundred rifles
          and guns. Shells were melted down
          to make bullets. A schoolteacher
          invented a way of making gunpowder,
          scraping shit off barn walls...

YOUNG GORKY hands the PHOTOGRAPHER SEVAN's smashed pocket
watch. It is splattered with blood.

Crying, YOUNG GORKY explains that SEVAN has been left in the
hands of the Turks. Words are not heard. YOUNG GORKY's
anguish is clear.

The PHOTOGRAPHER is stunned. After a moment, he picks up
the machine gun and goes running out of the shed.

                                              CUT TO:

39A   EXT. VAN. TURKEY. STREET. 1915 -- NIGHT

The camera follows the PHOTOGRAPHER as he goes rushing into
the main street of VAN, shooting his machine gun wildly in
every direction until he is shot dead by Turkish bullets.

                                              CUT TO:

40   INT. TORONTO AIRPORT. CUSTOMS STATION -- NIGHT

                    RAFFI
          They were heroes. What happened in
          Van in April of 1915 was an amazing
          act of self defense...like the Jews
          in the Warsaw ghetto. We hadn't
          done anything like that since we
          held back the Persians.

                    DAVID
          When did you hold back the Persians?

                    RAFFI
               (after a beat)
          451.

                    DAVID
          Fifteen hundred years before.

                    RAFFI
               (slight smile)
          Like I said. We go back.

Pause. DAVID stares at RAFFI. He takes a moment to leave
the story and get back to the matter at hand.

                         DAVID
               Can I see your passport?

RAFFI hands DAVID his passport. DAVID walks away, leaving
RAFFI alone to stare at the cans of film.

                                             CUT TO:

41   INT. STUDIO. JEVDET BEY'S OFFICE -- DAY

ALI is having publicity photographs taken as EDWARD stops
by.

                         EDWARD
               I wanted to thank you.

                         ALI
               Are you kidding? This was a huge
               break for me. You're one of my
               favorite directors. Thank you.

ALI and EDWARD shake hands. A moment as the two men look at
each other.

                         ALI (CONT'D)
               Can I ask something? Did you cast
               me just because I'm half Turkish?

                         EDWARD
               No. It was because I thought you
               would be perfect for the part.

                         ALI
               But being Turkish didn't hurt.

EDWARD smiles.

                         EDWARD
               No, it didn't hurt.

                         ALI
               You never asked me what I thought of
               the history.

                         EDWARD
               What is there to think?

                         ALI
               Whether I believe it happened. A
               genocide.

                         EDWARD
               I'm not sure it matters...

                         ALI
              Because when I'm playing a part,
              it's all supposed to come from here...
                   (he points to his
                    heart)
              And not from here...
                   (he points to his
                    head)
              Right?

                         EDWARD
                   (gravely)
              Yes.

RAFFI arrives to pick up ALI for his drive home. He overhears
the conversation between ALI and EDWARD.

                         ALI
              I think the Turks had real reason to
              believe the Armenians were a threat
              to their security. Their eastern
              border was threatened by Russia, and
              they were afraid the Armenians would
              betray them. It was war. Populations
              get moved around all the time.

EDWARD stares at ALI, then decides not to answer.

                         EDWARD
              Again, thank you for your work.

EDWARD leaves. RAFFI looks at ALI.

                         ALI
              I'll be a minute.

RAFFI nods, and chases after EDWARD.

                                                      CUT TO:

42   INT. STUDIO -- DAY

RAFFI catches up to EDWARD.

                         RAFFI
              Mr. Saroyan?

                         EDWARD
              Yes.

                         RAFFI
              Why didn't you answer him?

                         EDWARD
          He's having regrets about playing
          the part. I understand. He will
          receive anger from his people.

                         RAFFI
          But he thinks that Turkey was at <u>war</u>
          with Armenia. Why didn't you <u>explain</u>
          that the Armenians were Turkish
          <u>citizens</u>? That they had a right to
          be protected. It was ethnic
          cleansing. Mass murder.
               (pause, EDWARD waits)
          Doesn't it bother you that he doesn't
          get the history?

                         EDWARD
          Not really.

                         RAFFI
          Why not?

                         EDWARD
          Because <u>he</u> is history. His part is
          over.

RAFFI stares at EDWARD, wanting more.

                         EDWARD (CONT'D)
          Are you driving him home?

                         RAFFI
          Yes.

EDWARD reaches into his pocket and pulls out a wallet. He
hands RAFFI some money.

                         EDWARD
          Buy him a bottle of champagne. Let
          him think he's done something special.

EDWARD is about to leave. He stops, then returns back to
the confused RAFFI.

                         EDWARD (CONT'D)
          Do you know what still causes so
          much pain? It is not the people we
          lost, or the land. It's to know
          that we could be so hated. Who were
          these people who could hate us so
          much? How can they still deny their
          hatred, and so hate us even more?

                                                  CUT TO:

43   INT/EXT. RAFFI'S CAR. STREET. NEAR ALI'S APARTEMT -- DAY

RAFFI is driving ALI back from the studio.

>   RAFFI
>   That was a good scene.

>   ALI
>   Thanks.

>   RAFFI
>   It must be really weird to get into
>   that...head space.

>   ALI
>   Yeah.

>   RAFFI
>   I mean, I was raised with all these
>   stories, evil Turks and everything,
>   so I'm a little hardened to it all.
>   But what you did today...it made me
>   feel all that anger again.

>   ALI
>   Hey...thanks.

Pause. They have come to a stop. ALI pauses before getting
out.

>   ALI (CONT'D)
>   So...I guess you're Armenian.

>   RAFFI
>   Yes. That's what I mean when I said
>   I was raised to feel a lot of hatred
>   to...the person you're playing.

>   ALI
>   Right.

>   RAFFI
>   And you really pulled it off.

>   ALI
>   I guess it'd be hard to disappoint
>   you.

>   RAFFI
>   What do you mean?

>   ALI
>   Well, you've been kind of prepared
>   to hate my character. Like you said.

>   RAFFI
>   Sure, but I'm also kind of suspicious
>   of stuff that's <u>supposed</u> to make me
>   feel anything. Do you know what I
>   mean?

>   ALI
>   I think so.

>   RAFFI
>   So when I was watching you today,
>   even though I know you were <u>supposed</u>
>   to make me feel like hating you, I
>   really resisted it. But then, by
>   the end of the scene, I kind of felt
>   like...

ALI lets out a short laugh.

>   ALI
>   Killing me.

RAFFI is a little hurt and confused by ALI's statement.

>   RAFFI
>   Well, yes.

ALI laughs nervously.

>   RAFFI (CONT'D)
>   My Dad was killed trying to
>   assassinate a Turkish diplomat.
>   Almost fifteen years ago. I could
>   never understand what would make him
>   want to murder, what he had to imagine
>   that Turkish ambassador represented.
>   Today, you gave me a sense of what
>   was going on in his head. And I
>   want to thank you.

>   ALI
>   (uneasy)
>   You're...you're welcome.

                                              CUT TO:

44   EXT. ALI'S APARTMENT -- DAY

ALI leaves the car and opens the door to his apartment.
RAFFI seems frozen in his seat. He suddenly remembers the
champagne, and rushes out of the car, following ALI into his
building.

                                              CUT TO:

44A   INT. ALI'S APARTMENT -- DAY

RAFFI catches up to ALI in the hallway, offering him the
bottle of champagne.

                    ALI
          What's this?

                    RAFFI
          It's from Edward. He wanted to give
          it to you. In thanks.

                    ALI
          Was this before or after our
          conversation?

                    RAFFI
          After. I guess he wanted to show
          that there were no...hard feelings.

                    ALI
          Thanks.

                    RAFFI
          Were you serious about what you told
          him? That you don't think it
          happened?

                    ALI
          A genocide?

                    RAFFI
          Yes.

ALI smiles.

                    ALI
          Are you going to shoot me or
          something?

RAFFI shakes his head. His expression is intense. He needs
an answer.

                    ALI (CONT'D)
          Look, I never heard about any of
          this as I was growing up. I did
          some research for the part, and from
          what I've read...there were
          deportations. Lots of people died.
          Armenians and Turks. It was World
          War One.

                    RAFFI
          But Turkey wasn't at war with the
          Armenians, just like Germany wasn't
          at war with the Jews. They were
          Turkish citizens, expecting to be
          protected. The scene you just shot
          is based on an eyewitness account.
          Your character, Jevdet Bey, was placed
          in Van to carry out the complete
          elimination of the Armenian race.
          There were telegrams, communiques...

                    ALI
          I'm not saying something didn't
          happen.

                    RAFFI
          'Something'?

ALI holds up the bottle of champagne.

                    ALI
          Look, I was born here, and so were
          you. Right?

RAFFI nods.

                    ALI (CONT'D)
          It's a new country. So let's drop
          the fucking history, and get on with
          it. No-one's gonna wreck your home.
          No-one's gonna destroy your family.
          So let's go inside, uncork this, and
          celebrate.

ALI holds the champagne bottle up and smiles. RAFFI seems
frozen, then begins to speak...

                    RAFFI
          Looking at a map of rail lines to
          Dachau, Auschwitz, Treblinka, they
          must have thought, 'There's no bloody
          way we'll ever get away with this'...

ALI lowers the bottle only a little, still hopeful.

                    RAFFI (CONT'D)
          Do you know what Adolf Hitler told
          his military commanders, to convince
          them that his plan would work?

ALI stares at RAFFI.

                    RAFFI (CONT'D)
          'Who remembers the extermination of
          the Armenians?'

ALI approaches RAFFI, takes his head in his hand, and whispers
into his ear.

                    ALI
          And no one did.

ALI stares at RAFFI, a slight, ambiguous smile on his lips.
He turns to leave.

                                             CUT TO:

45   INT. WAREHOUSE -- DAY

RAFFI enters the warehouse. CELIA is finishing a deal with
some of her well-dressed clients. RAFFI moves away from
this group as CELIA says goodbye and closes the door behind
them. CELIA senses that RAFFI is disturbed.

                    CELIA
          What's the matter?

                    RAFFI
          That day when we walked out of my
          mother's lecture...

                    CELIA
          Yes?

                    RAFFI
          Why did you bring up my Dad?

                    CELIA
          Did I?
             (she smiles)
          I like the way you remember every
          word I say.

                    RAFFI
          You mentioned the effect of his
          absence...

                    CELIA
          Something like that.

                    RAFFI
          I don't understand how you can bring
          such a huge issue up, then be so
          casual about it.
                    (MORE)

RAFFI (CONT'D)
I mean, whenever we talk about
something that's happened to you,
it's always so mysterious and complex.

CELIA
Maybe that's what you feel. The
stuff that's happened to me <u>is</u>
mysterious and complex.

RAFFI
Why should I feel that?

CELIA moves up to RAFFI. Her sexuality is overwhelming.

CELIA
Because you love me.

RAFFI
I don't get it.

CELIA
You need to believe the stuff that's
happened to me makes me special.
It's a chemical thing.

RAFFI
Are you joking?

CELIA
A little.

RAFFI
If I want to be with you, I have to
reject everything about where I'm
from.

CELIA
(this is obvious)
Yes...?

RAFFI
But <u>you</u> don't.

CELIA
Raffi, I'm saying that what happened
to my father mattered. It <u>needs</u> to
matter.

RAFFI
How do <u>I</u> make it matter? What
happened to <u>my</u> father?

                         CELIA
             You just do.

                         RAFFI
             How?

                         CELIA
             How. You go there.

                         RAFFI
             Where?

                         CELIA
             Where they cut you down.

CELIA has unbuttoned RAFFI's shirt. She begins to kiss his
neck.

                         CELIA (CONT'D)
             And you stick it in here.

CELIA places her hand on his chest.

                         CELIA (CONT'D)
             And you listen to it beat. Beat all
             night, all day. That way, you never
             forget.

RAFFI is completely intoxicated by CELIA's caress.

                                                       CUT TO:

46   INT. TORONTO AIRPORT. CUSTOMS STATION -- NIGHT

RAFFI is lost in thought. DAVID comes walking back from
another office.

                         DAVID
             The number on this paper is
             disconnected.

                         RAFFI
             They must have closed the production
             office.

                         DAVID
             Then who's paying your bills?

                         RAFFI
             What bills?

                         DAVID
             The cost of your travel?

                    RAFFI
          I'm paying for it myself.

                    DAVID
          I thought it was for this film.

                    RAFFI
          It is.

                    DAVID
          So why wouldn't they be paying for
          it?

                    RAFFI
          Because they don't know I went.

Pause. DAVID waits for an explanation.

                    RAFFI (CONT'D)
          They didn't want to film there, so I
          went myself. I found a cameraman,
          and we went to shoot this material.

RAFFI sees that DAVID isn't convinced.

                    RAFFI (CONT'D)
          I thought that the director might
          need some extra shots. Stuff he
          might be able to cut in.

                    DAVID
          What about the digital effects? The
          people marching?

                    RAFFI
          That can still be added. If that's
          what they want to do.

DAVID looks at RAFFI's arms.

                    DAVID
          Roll up your sleeves.

                    RAFFI
          Why?

                    DAVID
          Please roll up your sleeves.

RAFFI does. DAVID checks for any evidence of needlemarks.

                    RAFFI
          I don't use drugs.

DAVID notices a digital video camera in the bag. He also finds a cache of tapes, each marked with a date.

>   DAVID
>   Can these be played back on this?

DAVID indicates the camera.

>   RAFFI
>   Yes.

>   DAVID
>   Could you put one on?

>   RAFFI
>   They're personal.

>   DAVID
>   So let's go somewhere private.

>   CUT TO:

47   INT. ART GALLERY. GORKY EXHIBITION -- DAY

PHILIP is walking through a gallery. He notices a young woman standing very close to a painting. He approaches her.

>   PHILIP
>   Excuse me. Please don't get too
>   close to the paintings.

The young woman pulls away. PHILIP recognizes CELIA from the evening of ANI's lecture.

>   CELIA
>   I like looking at the detail.

CELIA is looking at GORKY's painting, 'The Artist and His Mother'

>   CELIA (CONT'D)
>   Do you know anything about this
>   artist?

>   PHILIP
>   Not really. I mean, I picked up a
>   little from the lecture that lady
>   gave...the other night.

>   CELIA
>   Right.

>   PHILIP
>   The one you left.

                    CELIA
     What do you remember from the lecture?

                    PHILIP
     How much he suffered. Losing his
     family. His mother dying of
     starvation in his arms...

                    CELIA
     His pain.

                    PHILIP
     Yes.

                    CELIA
     How his pain made him paint this
     way.

                    PHILIP
     That's...right.

                    CELIA
     When you look at this painting, can
     you understand?

                    PHILIP
     Understand...what?

                    CELIA
     That he would kill himself.

CELIA runs her hand around her neck. PHILIP is slightly on
edge, feeling CELIA's unpredictable energy.

                    CELIA (CONT'D)
     His home was lost, his land destroyed,
     his people murdered. This painting
     shows us pain. So much pain he
     couldn't stand it.

CELIA walks away. PHILIP watches her, jarred by the intensity
of this meeting.

                                                   CUT TO:

48   EXT. ANI -- DAY

A video image of the beautiful ruins on ANI. The destroyed
churches. Over these emotionally charged images, RAFFI
recites a letter to his mother.

>   RAFFI
>   (voice over)
>   I'm here, Mom. Ani. In a dream
>   world, the three of us would be here
>   together. Dad, you and me. I
>   remember all the stories I used to
>   hear about this place, the glorious
>   capital of our kingdom. Ancient
>   history. Like the story that Dad
>   was a freedom fighter, fighting
>   for...the return of this, I guess.

                                                    CUT TO:

49   INT. TORONTO AIRPORT. OFFICE AREA -- NIGHT

As the video letter goes on, the scene shifts to an office
area at the airport where DAVID watches the digital footage
on the screen of a small camera that RAFFI has shot it on.

>   RAFFI
>   (his voice continuing
>   on the tape)
>   What am I supposed to feel when I
>   look at these ruins? Do I believe
>   that they're ravaged by time, or do
>   I believe that they've been willfully
>   destroyed? Is this proof of what
>   happened? Am I supposed to feel
>   anger? Can I ever feel the anger
>   that Dad must have felt when...

RAFFI turns the tape off.

>   DAVID
>   (finishing the thought)
>   When he tried to kill a Turkish
>   diplomat.

RAFFI is stunned.

>   RAFFI
>   How did you know?

>   DAVID
>   You gave me your passport. Files
>   are kept. You happen to be the son
>   of a terrorist.

DAVID takes the camera away from RAFFI.

>   DAVID (CONT'D)
>   How do I turn this back on?

RAFFI shows him. The tape continues.

> RAFFI
> (on the tape)
> ...he tried to kill that man. Why
> was he prepared to give us up for
> that, Mom? What's the legacy he's
> supposed to have given me? Why can't
> I take any comfort in his death?

                                        CUT TO:

50 EXT. TURKEY -- DAY

A deserted plain. A ruined church. Scorching heat.

> RAFFI
> (his voice continuing
> on the tape)
> When I see these places, I realize
> how much we've lost. Not just the
> land and the lives, but the loss of
> any way to remember it. There is
> nothing here to prove that anything
> ever happened.

As RAFFI's voice fades away, an image of hundreds of people
marching through this desert dissolves into view. The people
are haggard and broken.

The YOUNG GORKY is seen beside his MOTHER, who is on the
verge of exhaustion.

                                        CUT TO:

51 INT. ARSHILE GORKY'S STUDIO. NEW YORK CITY. 1935 -- DAY

Detail on the painting 'The Artist and His Mother'. The
camera drifts from the paintbrush hovering indecisively over
the blurred hand of the Mother, to a CLOSE-UP of GORKY's
face as he stares at the canvas.

GORKY seems troubled, lost in a bad memory.

                                        CUT TO:

52 EXT. VAN. TURKEY. STREET. PHOTORAPHER'S AREA. 1912 -- DAY

An image of SEVAN, handing YOUNG GORKY another flower to
hold in his hand as he poses for the portrait.

YOUNG GORKY's P.O.V. of his MOTHER's hands as they rest on
her lap against the apron.

SEVAN holds a reflector board. The sunlight beams
mysteriously onto SHUSHAN's hands.

CUT TO:

53   INT. STUDIO. MISSION SET -- DAY

ANI is looking at the previous scene being shown on a
television monitor. ROUBEN is beside her on a cell phone.

                ROUBEN
    Okay, I'll ask her. Just a second...

ROUBEN leans over to ANI.

                ROUBEN (CONT'D)
    The publicist wants to know if it'd
    be okay if a news crew shows up at
    the reading. It'd be great promotion.

ANI is mesmerized by the image of GORKY on the monitor. She
nods.

                ROUBEN (CONT'D)
    Yes, she says that should be fine.
    Bye.

ROUBEN puts away the cell phone. He looks at the monitor.

                ROUBEN (CONT'D)
    What do you think?

                ANI
    He's amazing.

                ROUBEN
    I thought you'd be happy.

ROUBEN stares at ANI, and lifts her hand. ANI is surprised
by this gesture, but doesn't resist it.

ROUBEN leans over to kiss ANI, who remains watching the
screen. ROUBEN pulls back.

                ROUBEN (CONT'D)
    Is this okay?

                ANI
    I told you. He's amazing.
      (beat, she realizes)
    Oh this. Sure.

ANGLE ON

A CLOSE-UP on the monitor of the actor playing GORKY.

                                              CUT TO:

54   EXT. VAN. TURKEY. STREET. 1915 -- NIGHT

YOUNG GORKY watches a Turkish soldier being shot. He leaves
his protected position, and runs through the street. As he
approaches the body of the Turkish soldier, he begins to
strip it of its weapons, finally tugging at the rifle. As
bullets fly around him, YOUNG GORKY realizes that the soldier
is still alive. He smiles weakly at the boy. YOUNG GORKY
runs back to his position with the captured gun.

                    ANI (V.O.)
               As a boy involved in the heroic
               defense of Van, Gorky was witness to
               one of the most courageous moments
               in Armenian history... Thousands of
               Turkish troops armed with the most
               powerful artillery against a few
               hundred men with ancient guns...

                                              CUT TO:

55   INT. ART GALLERY. BOOKSTORE -- DAY

ANI is reading from her book to a well-attended event at a
large bookstore. A television crew is filming this. ROUBEN
is beside the camera.

                    ANI
                 (reading from her
                  book)
               But the years which were to follow
               would see him lose a home, his people,
               and - most traumatically - his beloved
               mother.

CLOSE-UP of the painting from the dust jacket of the book.

                    ANI (CONT'D)
               Gorky's memories of those years
               threatened to overwhelm him. In his
               most famous painting, Gorky leaves
               his mother's hand unfinished, as if
               the history of its composition, like
               that of his people, had been violently
               interrupted. The earthly sensuality
               of the mother's touch is no more.
               Only a pure, burning spiritual light
               remains...

CELIA is holding this copy of the book, staring at the detail of the painting on the cover. She suddenly comes forward as the video camera swings around to find her.

                    CELIA
          You said before that Gorky worked on
          that painting ten years.

ANI tries to respond to CELIA's questions in a cool manner.

                    ANI
          That's right.

                    CELIA
          Is it possible to work on something
          that long and leave it unfinished?

                    ANI
          The painting is finished. The
          unfinished hands of his mother were
          purposely left that way.

                    CELIA
          Isn't it more likely that he finished
          his mother's hands, then decided to
          erase them? That he needed to destroy
          what he made?

                    ANI
          No. Destruction is part of the
          painting. It mirrors the history of
          the artist's people.

ANI is silent. ROUBEN is whispering something into the cameraman's ear, who is recording all this.

                    CELIA
          Can we talk about his suicide?

                    ANI
          No.

                    CELIA
          Why not?

                    ANI
          Because it was not...what I was
          planning to read.

                    CELIA
          I'm just curious about the way you
          describe the suicide in your book.
                    (MORE)

                    CELIA (CONT'D)
          You make it sound as if Gorky was
          flooded with memories of the Genocide,
          but you don't talk about the role of
          his wife.

ANI remains frozen.

                    ANI
          Thank you all for coming to this
          event.

ANI begins to walk away.

                    CELIA
          Gorky's wife was having an affair
          with his best friend. He adored
          her, and she betrayed him. He killed
          himself because of his wife's
          confession...

ANI grabs CELIA by the arm, and leads her to a section of
the bookstore where they are relatively alone.

                    ANI
          What the fuck is wrong with you?

                    CELIA
          You said something to my father.

                    ANI
          Said what?

                    CELIA
          That you were having an affair.

                    ANI
          He tripped and fell.

                    CELIA
          You cut his heart.

                    ANI
          He tripped and fell.

                    CELIA
          You were going to leave him. A man
          who gave up everything to be with
          you! Who left my mother...

                    ANI
          He tripped and fell.

                        CELIA
                (in Quebecois French)
            He adored you. If he knew that you
            were going to leave, he would have
            killed himself.

                                            CUT TO:

56   EXT. NORTHERN QUEBEC -- DAY

        CLOSE-UP on ANI's face as she talks to an out-of-focus male
        figure in the background (CELIA's FATHER). The camera follows
        ANI's face as she continues to speak, her eyes averted away
        from the male figure behind her.

        As ANI turns away from this figure, the camera loses him in
        the frame, focusing on ANI as she speaks an unheard
        confession. Her lips move with no sound. Male breaths are
        heard exaggerated on the sound track.

        At a certain point, ANI's lips stop moving, and she turns
        around to see her partner's response to the news she has
        given him.

        The sound of breathing stops.

        The male figure is nowhere to be seen.

        ANI looks for him in panic. She looks at the cliff edge.

                        ANI (V.O.)
            I didn't see him fall.

                        CELIA (V.O.)
                    (in French)
            He jumped!

                                            CUT TO:

57   INT. ART GALLERY. BOOKSTORE -- DAY

        ANI grabs CELIA by the arm.

                        ANI
            I won't remember!

                        CELIA
                    (in French)
            You won't remember?!

                        ANI
            I can't! I won't!

                         CELIA
                      (in French)
               Why not?

ANI suddenly looks at CELIA with resolve and composure,
responding in perfect Parisian French...

                         ANI
               I can't remember it the way you want
               me to. And even if I could remember
               what you want me to remember, I
               won't. I can't afford to. I don't
               need to.

CELIA stares at ANI, stunned, then turns to leave. The video
team, directed by ROUBEN, follows her.

                                             CUT TO:

57A   INT. ART GALLERY. LOBBY -- DAY

      CELIA rushes past the admissions desk into the gallery...

                                             CUT TO:

58   INT. ART GALLERY. GORKY EXHIBITION -- DAY

      CELIA, distraught, is moving through the gallery towards
      Gorky's painting 'The Artist and His Mother'. PHILIP notices
      her, and begins to follow.

      ROUBEN is running behind, catching up with the video
      cameraman. This is all being recorded.

      CELIA is in front of the painting. She takes out a knife,
      and slashes the painting. PHILIP hurls himself at her, but
      it is too late.

      The painting is damaged.

      In the ensuing struggle to gain control, PHILIP is
      accidentally stabbed.

                                             CUT TO:

59   INT. TORONTO AIRPORT. OFFICE AREA -- NIGHT

      DAVID is staring at RAFFI, who has just told him something.

                         DAVID
               Was it an accident?

      RAFFI nods.

                    DAVID (CONT'D)
But she was carrying a knife.

                    RAFFI
Yes.

                    DAVID
So there was a degree
of...premeditation.

                    RAFFI
It was a pocket knife. Something
she always carries.

                    DAVID
Because she never knows when she
might need it.

                    RAFFI
What do you mean?

                    DAVID
I'm talking about her job. What she
did for a living.

RAFFI stares at DAVID.

                    DAVID (CONT'D)
I know all sorts of things. When
she was arrested, the police
discovered she dealt drugs, as well
as various credit frauds on the net.
You were questioned about your
involvement. She insisted that you
had nothing to do with it. It's all
on your files. Is that true?

                    RAFFI
What?

                    DAVID
That you had nothing to do with it?

                    RAFFI
I...knew about it.

                    DAVID
And you didn't tell anyone?

                    RAFFI
No.

                    DAVID
          So you didn't have a problem with
          the fact that your sister was dealing
          in drugs.

                    RAFFI
          Step-sister.

                    DAVID
          Oh. Yes. Step-sister.

Pause. DAVID stares hard at RAFFI.

                    DAVID (CONT'D)
          Most people are obvious about the
          crimes they commit. By the time I
          get them to this room, it's just a
          matter of time before it comes out.

                    RAFFI
          What?

                    DAVID
          The shit.

                    RAFFI
          I...I don't understand.

DAVID moves to the elevated toilet in the corner of the room.

                    DAVID
          My job becomes pretty simple. I sit
          where you are and watch them on this
          toilet. Waiting for the truth. The
          compressed tablets of heroin.
          Sometimes they get so nervous that
          the body acid breaks the package and
          they overdose. But that can take
          hours. I sit and wait. Usually
          it's pretty silent. They have time
          to think. So do I. You know what
          goes through my mind, Raffi?

RAFFI shakes his head.

                    DAVID (CONT'D)
          I wonder if I feel sorry for them.
          They're usually kids. Around your
          age. I'm about to destroy their
          lives. I know that they're sorry
          for what they've done. They would
          never go through this again. But
          the action has been taken. It's too
          late.

                        RAFFI
          I...I had to go there.

                        DAVID
          I have no doubt about that. A flame
          was lit in your heart. You thought
          things would be clarified by going
          there, but they weren't. You lost
          meaning. People are vulnerable when
          they lose meaning. They do stupid
          things.

                                        CUT TO:

60   INT. STUDIO. MISSION SET -- DAY

      ROUBEN is following ANI as she walks towards the set.

                        ROUBEN
                  (agitated and excited)
          Ani, you're being ridiculous. Her
          attacking the painting had nothing
          to do with this film.

                        ANI
          I can't go on with this.

                        ROUBEN
          You need to. We all do.

      ANI suddenly stops and stares at ROUBEN.

                        ANI
          What does it mean to you?

                        ROUBEN
          I've been working on this for five
          years.

                        ANI
          Not the film. What happened today?

                        ROUBEN
          I...I'm sickened by it.

                        ANI
          Because you feel responsible?

                        ROUBEN
          Of course not. I feel sickened
          because...because I don't think people
          should do those things.

                    ANI
          Attack works of art?

                    ROUBEN
          Right.

                    ANI
          And guess what? People aren't <u>allowed</u>
          to do those things, just like they're
          not <u>allowed</u> to steal cars, or kill
          their neighbors, or...

                    ROUBEN
          What's your point, Ani?

                    ANI
          My point is that you're not sickened
          because people shouldn't 'do those
          things'. Because they <u>do</u>. They do
          them all the time. What you're
          sickened by is that it was that
          <u>particular</u> painting. You're sickened
          because that painting is a repository
          of our history. It's a sacred code
          that explains who we are, and how
          and why we got here.

ANI breaks away from ROUBEN. She proceeds to the active
set. Off lens, the action is cut as an assistant director
approaches ANI.

                    ASSISTANT
          We're rolling.

                    ANI
          I need to speak to Edward.

                    ASSISTANT
          That's impossible.

ANI proceeds undeterred onto the set. It is a crowded scene
with starving extras huddled around MARTIN, playing USSHER,
heroically trying to save a young child's life. Blood is
gushing from the child's wounds. Ussher is splattered in
blood.

                    MARTIN
                (in character)
          I need a clamp!

ANI confronts EDWARD.

                    ANI
          I need to talk with you.

                    EDWARD
          We're shooting a scene.

MARTIN slowly comes out of character as he understands the
violence of the intrusion.

                    MARTIN
               (emerging from a trance)
          What...is this? We're besieged by
          Turks, we've run out of supplies,
          and most of us will die. The crowd
          needs a miracle. This child is
          bleeding to death. If I can save
          his life, it will give us the spirit
          to continue.

MARTIN points to a woman, still in character, sobbing as she
holds her child's hand.

                    MARTIN (CONT'D)
          This is his mother. She's seen the
          rest of her family massacred. Her
          pregnant daughter was raped in front
          of her eyes, just before her stomach
          was slashed open to stab her unborn
          child. Her husband had his testicles
          cut off and stuffed into his mouth.
               (to ANI)
          Who the fuck are you?

ANI is stunned by MARTIN's vitriol. She backs down from the
bright lights.

                                        CUT TO:

61   INT. STUDIO. -- DAY

EDWARD and ROUBEN are having a conversation in another part
of the studio.

                    EDWARD
          I don't understand. Why does she
          think it has anything to do with the
          film?

                    ROUBEN
          She's confused.

                    EDWARD
          About what?

                         ROUBEN
          Edward, do you remember that time we
          went to hear the lecture? The woman
          who confronted her, the one you told
          to be quiet? It's the same person.
          It's her step-daughter.

                         EDWARD
          She attacked the painting?

                         ROUBEN
          Yes.

EDWARD turns to look at ANI in the distance. She is in front
of another set, talking with someone. It is the set for
GORKY's studio in New York in 1935.

                                                    CUT TO:

62   INT. ARSHILE GORKY'S STUDIO. NEW YORK CITY. 1935 -- DAY

The studio set of ARSHILE GORKY's studio. ANI and the actor
playing GORKY are having a conversation in Armenian.

                         ANI
          What's the matter?

                         GORKY
          I feel this is all a cruel joke.
          This man heard you give a lecture.
          He got excited about fitting Gorky
          into his film. The coincidence over
          my childhood and the history he wanted
          to tell are irresistible. But the
          truth is that I don't need to be in
          this.

                         ANI
          That's not true.

                         GORKY
          What is true? My meaningful stares
          at the canvas I am painting, the
          picture I am looking at? I am
          conjured for a few days of shooting,
          then I will be discarded. No other
          artist has suffered what I have.
          Now my life is reduced to a few scenes
          in a movie about someone else.

GORKY leaves the frame, leaving ANI alone. EDWARD and ROUBEN
approach her from the background.

                    EDWARD
          Ani, Rouben has explained the
          situation to me.

                    ROUBEN
          We understand how upset you must be
          about the painting...

                    ANI
          I'm letting it get the better of me.
               (beat)
          Except I don't know where the better
          of me is anymore.

                    ROUBEN
          The best thing about all of us has
          to be invested in this film.

                    EDWARD
          Rouben is right. We must work
          together.

                    ANI
          And the painting?

                    EDWARD
          It will be repaired.

                    ROUBEN
          Like nothing happened.

                    ANI
          Except it did.

     EDWARD looks at ANI with calm and reassurance.

                                             CUT TO:

63   INT. ALI'S APARTMENT. LIVING/DINING AREA -- DAY

     PHILIP is resting on his couch, recovering from the attack.
     He is reading a story to TONY, who sits beside him. ALI is
     doing some work in the background.

                    PHILIP
               (reading from the
                story book)
          ...Noah explained, You must come
          with us. Or you will perish in the
          flood. But the unicorn only laughed,
          and ran off to play. Clouds began
          to darken the sky. The sun
          disappeared. And the rains came...

PHILIP closes the book as ALI enters the room.

                    PHILIP (CONT'D)
          (to TONY)
So you see? There <u>were</u> single animals
invited on the Ark.

                    TONY
What do you mean?

                    PHILIP
Well, there was only <u>one</u> unicorn.

                    TONY
          (confused)
But he didn't go.

                    PHILIP
He was still asked.

TONY thinks about this. ALI doesn't entirely approve of
PHILIP's tactic.

                    ALI
I better drop him off.

                                      CUT TO:

64   EXT. JANET'S HOUSE. STREET -- DAY

ALI is walking TONY back to JANET's house.

                    TONY
Was Daddy right?

                    ALI
About what?

                    TONY
That there was only one unicorn?

                    ALI
          (evasive)
I...I'm not sure.

                    TONY
Because at the beginning of the book,
there was a picture of two unicorns
playing.

                    ALI
          (unsure)
Well, maybe the second unicorn
was...imaginary. Or something.

> TONY
> Like it wasn't really there?

ALI suddenly bends down and addresses the matter.

> ALI
> Look, your Dad thinks that by telling
> you the story of the Unicorn, it's
> going to make you feel better about
> us.

> TONY
> Why?

> ALI
> It'll make you feel that the way we
> live is okay.

> TONY
> But I know that it's okay. Noah had
> to take a male and female because
> they had to make babies. That's
> all.

ALI smiles at TONY, astonished by the maturity of his
response. Before he can formulate an answer, the door opens
and TONY goes inside.

                                          CUT TO:

65   EXT. AGHTAMAR -- DAY

A video image of a detail from the church. A stone carving
of Madonna and Child.

> RAFFI
> (voice over)
> You're right. This is the inspiration
> of his painting. It's in the eyes.
> Their gaze. I remember you saying
> that Gorky's mother would bring him
> here when he was a little boy.

The video camera zooms into a detail of the stone carving...

> RAFFI (CONT'D)
> How could he ever think of what he
> saw here and not remember his mother's
> hands?

                                          CUT TO:

66   INT. TORONTO AIRPORT. OFFICE AREA -- NIGHT

DAVID is watching the digital images.

                    DAVID
          Does she know you went there?

                    RAFFI
          Who?

                    DAVID
          Your mother?

                    RAFFI
          To the island? No, not yet.

                    DAVID
          You haven't spoken to her.

                    RAFFI
          No.

                    DAVID
              (a far away smile)
          People lose touch.

DAVID is lost in his thoughts of PHILIP. His expression is
noticed by RAFFI.

                    RAFFI
          There's something I've been meaning
          to ask you.

                    DAVID
          Yes?

                    RAFFI
          Aren't there dogs you use for this
          sort of thing?

                    DAVID
          What sort of thing?

                    RAFFI
          If you think there are drugs in these
          cans.

                    DAVID
          Yes, we do have dogs for that.

Long pause. DAVID watches the videotape.

                    RAFFI
          So...why don't you use one?

                    DAVID
          What?

                    RAFFI
          A dog.

                    DAVID
          A dog would take away what I like
          most about this job.

                    RAFFI
               (beat)
          What's that?

                    DAVID
          The opportunity to better understand
          how the mind works. A dog would
          come in and bark. That bark can
          only mean one thing. There are drugs
          in these cans.

DAVID suddenly barks.

                    DAVID (CONT'D)
          'You're lying! I caught you! You're
          a liar!'

Pause.

                    DAVID (CONT'D)
          That's what a dog does.

                    RAFFI
               (beat)
          Right.

                    DAVID
          I'm not saying that what a dog does
          isn't important. But there other
          issues involved, aren't there? Things
          a dog doesn't have the capacity to
          consider.

Pause.

                    DAVID (CONT'D)
          Is someone picking you up?

                    RAFFI
          No.

                    DAVID
          That's good. They'd be worried.
               (MORE)

                         DAVID (CONT'D)
               (beat)
          Even I'm worried.

                         RAFFI
          About what?

                         DAVID
          About you. What are we going to do?
          There's no one for me to contact, no
          way of confirming that a single word
          you've told me tonight is true.

                         RAFFI
          You don't believe me?

                                             CUT TO:

67   INT. STUDIO. MISSION SET -- DAY

In his room at the American mission in Van, USSHER, played
by MARTIN, is checking the temperature of the young boy whose
life he has saved. He moves through his room, crowded with
medical supplies, and moves outside to the balcony

                    MARTIN AS USSHER
               (voice over)
          In a field of cinders where Armenian
          life was still dying, a German woman,
          trying not to cry, told me the horror
          she witnessed...

                                             CUT TO:

68   INT. STUDIO. MISSION SET -- DAY

A few days before, A German woman sits in front of USSHER.
She recounts her story as USSHER continues his voice over...

                    MARTIN AS USSHER (V.O.)
          "I must tell you what I saw, so people
          will understand the crimes men do to
          men. It was Sunday morning, the
          first useless Sunday dawning on the
          corpses. I went to the balcony of
          my window, and saw a dark crowd in
          the courtyard lashing a group of
          young women...

                                             CUT TO:

69   EXT. STUDIO. MISSION SET -- DAY

From her window, the German woman witnesses the following
scene...

                    MARTIN AS USSHER
                (continuing his voice
                  over entry)
            An animal of a man shouted, "You
            must dance, dance when the drum
            beats!" With fury the whips cracked
            on the flesh of the women. Hand in
            hand the brides began their circle
            dance...

The camera floats above this grisly scene.

                    MARTIN AS USSHER (CONT'D)
            "Dance!", they raved, "Dance till
            you die, dance with bare breasts,
            without shame..."

One of the women is stripped naked.

                    MARTIN AS USSHER (CONT'D)
            The women collapsed. "Get up!", the
            crowd screamed, brandishing their
            swords. Then someone brought a jug
            of kerosene. The brides were
            anointed. "Dance!", they thundered,
            "Here's a fragrance sweeter than any
            perfume."

One of the men in the distance approaches the gas-soaked
women with a flaming torch. It is thrown at the terrified
women.

                                                    CUT TO:

70   INT. STUDIO -- DAY

MARTIN is recording a voice over. He can barely contain his
emotion as he finishes the recording of the story.

                    MARTIN AS USSHER
            With a torch they set the naked brides
            on fire. And the charred bodies
            rolled and tumbled to their deaths.

MARTIN takes a pause, then continues.

                    MARTIN AS USSHER (CONT'D)
              The German woman looked at me and
              said, "How shall I dig out these
              eyes of mine? Tell me, how?"

The camera moves away from MARTIN to find EDWARD behind the
mixing board. EDWARD's expression is full of emotion as he
watches the next image on the screen...

                                                  CUT TO:

71   EXT. VAN. TURKEY. COUNTRY. RIVERBANK -- DAY

A horrifying image. A crowd of people are being lead into
the banks of a river, where a group of Turkish guards is
shooting at them. The people plead for mercy, as they fall
into the bloody waters.

The camera tracks along this mass of dead bodies until it
arrives at a cart where a Turkish soldier is raping a young
woman. The camera moves close to the anguished woman's arm,
following it down to her hand.

The young mother is holding the hand of her terrified eight
year old girl, who is hiding underneath the cart. The girl
is fighting back her tears, trying to comfort her mother by
kissing her fingers while she is savaged above her.

                         EDWARD (V.O.)
              My mother never talked about what
              happened during the march. Only one
              story...

                                                  CUT TO:

72   INT. LIMOUSINE. -- NIGHT

ANI is riding in a stretch limousine. She is dressed for a
glamorous event. She is seated beside ROUBEN.

On the opposite side of the limo, EDWARD takes out a small
pill box full of the pomegranate seeds. He holds one up as
he explains the story to MARTIN, who sits beside him.

                         EDWARD
              They had a pomegranate tree in their
              garden. When they came to take the
              family away, she grabbed one of the
              fruits. She knew the journey would
              be long. Everyday, she would take
              out one seed, and eat it. She would
              bite it bit by bit, pretending that
              one seed was a whole meal.
                         (MORE)

                              EDWARD (CONT'D)
                         (slight pause)
                    Now, when I eat a pomegranate seed,
                    it brings me two things. Luck, and
                    the power to imagine.

EDWARD hands a seed to MARTIN, who is moved by the gift.
ANI's cell phone rings. She searches in her purse for the
phone.

                              EDWARD (CONT'D)
                    You'll remember to turn that off for
                    the screening.

ANI nods as she connects.

                              ANI
                    Hello?...Raffi? Where are you?

                                                            CUT TO:

73   INT. TORONTO AIRPORT. OFFICE AREA -- NIGHT

        DAVID watches as RAFFI talks to his mother.

                              RAFFI
                    Mom...hi...I just got back to
                    Toronto...Yes, I just got back.
                    They've stopped me here at customs
                    with all the footage that I shot for
                    the film. They're wondering what's
                    inside the cans...

                                                            CUT TO:

74   INT. LIMOUSINE -- NIGHT

        ANI is trying to contain her emotions as she talks to her
        son for the first time in months.

                              ANI
                    What cans? What are you talking
                    about...?

        ANGLE ON

        EDWARD as he listens to this conversation.

                                                            CUT TO:

75   INT. TORONTO AIRPORT. OFFICE AREA -- NIGHT

        RAFFI is pretending that his mother is saying something else
        as he speaks to her in front of DAVID.

                         RAFFI
          That's right. The stuff I had to
          shoot around Van. I've been stopped
          at customs with all these cans of
          film, and they want to open them up,
          but they can't...

                                             CUT TO:

76   INT. LIMOUSINE -- NIGHT

ANI looks at EDWARD as she speaks into her phone.

                         ANI
                    (in Armenian)
          Do you want me to lie, Raffi?...

                                             CUT TO:

77   INT. TORONTO AIRPORT. OFFICE AREA -- NIGHT

                         RAFFI
          Yes...I miss you too...There's so
          much to tell you...I went to Aghtamar,
          Mom...I saw the Mother and Child on
          the church...I had some days free so
          I went to Aghtamar...

                         ANI
          Aghtamar...

                         RAFFI
          Here, I'll let you speak to the
          inspector. He needs to know more
          about the film this is for...

RAFFI hands the phone over to DAVID.

                         DAVID
          Hello. You are Raffi's mother?

                         ANI
          Yes.

                         DAVID
          And you are a professor at the
          university?

                         ANI
          That's right.

                         DAVID
          And you were involved with this film?

                                              CUT TO:

78   INT. LIMOUSINE -- NIGHT

                         ANI
          Yes. As an historical consultant.
          A book I wrote was used as a
          reference...

                         DAVID
          What was the book about?

                         ANI
          It's about the life of Arshile Gorky.

                         DAVID
          Is that the main character in the
          film?

ANI stares at MARTIN.

                         ANI
          No. Does my son need a lawyer?

                         DAVID
          Not at the moment. What did your
          son have to shoot in Turkey?

                         ANI
          He...he had to go to the place where
          Gorky was born.

                         DAVID
          Why?

                         ANI
          To shoot some material.

EDWARD looks questioningly at ANI, who seems frozen.

                         DAVID
          And how would this material be used?

                         ANI
               (after a beat)
          To help show what happened.

                         DAVID
          How did he die?

                         ANI
              Who?

                         DAVID
              Gorky.

                         ANI
              Why are you asking me...?

                         DAVID
              Did he kill himself?

                                             CUT TO:

79   EXT. FILM THEATRE -- NIGHT

      The stretch limousine has pulled up to a red carpet. There
      is a large crowd there. It is a big event. The premiere of
      an important new film.

      The door of the limo is ceremoniously opened.

                                             CUT TO:

80   INT. LIMOUSINE -- NIGHT

      EDWARD tries to coax ANI.

                         EDWARD
              Ani, we have to go.

      The crowd is heard screaming for MARTIN. MARTIN leaves the
      limo, as the crowd swells to a roar.

                         EDWARD (CONT'D)
                    (in Armenian)
              We have to go.

                                             CUT TO:

81   INT. TORONTO AIRPORT. OFFICE AREA -- NIGHT

      DAVID hears the crowd over the phone.

                         DAVID
              Where are you?

                         ANI
              Where am I?

      ROUBEN grabs the phone from ANI, and speaks into it.

>   ROUBEN
>   She's at the premiere of the film
>   and now she has to go.

ANI grabs the phone back.

>   ANI
>   I need to speak to my son.

>   DAVID
>   Are you saying the film is <u>finished</u>?

>   ANI
>   Please, let me speak to my son.

DAVID hands the phone over. RAFFI holds it to his ear.

>   ANI (CONT'D)
>   Raffi?

>   RAFFI
>   Yes.

>   ANI
>   (in Armenian)
>   Tell me what to do.

>   RAFFI
>   Sure...I'll meet you at home.

>   CUT TO:

82   EXT/INT. FILM THEATRE -- NIGHT

ANI's heart is broken as she is grabbed by ROUBEN and pulled
from the limousine.

In a daze, she stares at the crowd in front of her. MARTIN
is surrounded by cameras and television crews trying to steal
his attention. EDWARD is also being interviewed.

ROUBEN is left alone, vulnerable by the lack of attention.

>   CUT TO:

83   INT. DETENTION CENTER -- DAY

A group of women are watching television in the communal
room of a prison/detention center. CELIA is watching the
program, an entertainment show broadcasting this clip from
the film premiere.

                              JOURNALIST
                    Marty, how are you responding to the
                    people who say this is all an
                    exaggeration?

                              MARTIN
                         (after a short beat)
                    This is all documented. Every word
                    I say is directly quoted from Ussher's
                    own journal.

                              JOURNALIST
                    What's more fun? Playing a hero or
                    a bad guy?

                              MARTIN
                    Well, I'd have to say that a bad
                    guy's 'funner'...

The show immediately cuts to action clips from the film.

                                                        CUT TO:

83A   EXT. VAN. TURKEY. STREET. 1915 -- DAY

In a scene from the film, an Armenian fighter makes a heroic
jump onto a Turkish soldier riding on horseback, bringing
him to the ground. The two men battle each other on the
ground.

                                                        CUT TO:

84   INT. FILM THEATRE -- NIGHT

MARTIN being taped by the same journalist. The moment is
repeated, the last comment put into a context that the
television audience will never see.

                              MARTIN
                    Well, I'd have to say that a bad
                    guy's 'funner'...but this isn't a
                    film about having fun. It's a film
                    about heroism. The heroism of a
                    man, and the heroism of a people...

                                                        CUT TO:

85   INT. DETENTION CENTER -- DAY

EDWARD being interviewed on the T.V. show.

                              JOURNALIST
                    Was it hard to get him to play a
                    'good guy'?

                              EDWARD
                Marty is a versatile...

                              JOURNALIST
                         (interrupting)
                Tell the <u>truth</u>.
                         (beat)
                What's more fun to direct? Good
                guys or bad guys?

ANGLE shifts to CELIA watching the television.

CELIA laughs, almost inadvertently.

A guard approaches CELIA from behind. She whispers something
to her. CELIA nods and gets up to leave the room.

                                             CUT TO:

86   INT. FILM THEATRE. LOBBY -- NIGHT

ANI is blocked by the jam of cameras around MARTIN and EDWARD.

ANI notices the actor playing GORKY, who has been left
completely alone. Something about his presence shocks her
into reality. She leaves ROUBEN, and begins to make her way
through the crowd.

                              ROUBEN
                Ani!

ANI rushes out of the theatre.

                                             CUT TO:

87   EXT. TURKEY -- DAY

A digital image, shot from a moving train, of Mount Ararat.

                                             CUT TO:

88   INT. TORONTO AIRPORT. OFFICE AREA -- NIGHT

RAFFI is showing this image to DAVID as he amends his story
nervously.

                              RAFFI
                See, I shot this on the way there.
                This is where I met them. On a train.

                              DAVID
                To Ararat.

                    RAFFI
          Yes, they were going to shoot a
          commercial. I became friends with
          the camera assistant. I told him
          that I wanted to get an image of the
          mountain.

                    DAVID
          Why?

                    RAFFI
          For the film. I thought it was
          something that could be used.

                    DAVID
          How? The film is finished.

                    RAFFI
          I wasn't thinking about that. Look,
          this is us driving up...

RAFFI fast-forwards to an image shot from the road, driving
up to the mountain peak.

                    RAFFI (CONT'D)
          He had to bribe a soldier to take us
          up. This is a military road. We
          went as high up as we could, then we
          shot this footage up there. On film.
          This film.

                    DAVID
          Why didn't you tell me this before?

                    RAFFI
          Because I needed to tell you the
          other story.

                    DAVID
          Why?

RAFFI is in tears.

                    RAFFI
          Because it meant something to me.

DAVID is resisting emotion. His reaction is disbelieving.

                    DAVID
          So this 'crew person' gave you the
          film, let you use his camera, bribed
          a soldier, and then drove you up the
          mountain?

> RAFFI
> Yes.

> DAVID
> Did he ask you to do <u>him</u> a favor?
> In return?

> RAFFI
> Who?

> DAVID
> Your friend.

RAFFI doesn't respond.

> DAVID (CONT'D)
> Raffi, did he ask you to bring
> anything into this country?

RAFFI, overcome with emotion and fear, nods.

> RAFFI
> Yes. He asked me to bring these.

RAFFI points to the cans.

> DAVID
> What's in them?

> RAFFI
> He said it's film.

> DAVID
> Where's it going?

> RAFFI
> He gave me a number.
> (beat)
> This is the truth.

CUT TO:

89   INT. FILM THEATRE -- NIGHT

Projected on the screen, an emotionally loaded scene ripples
through the packed theatre. EDWARD and ROUBEN stare at the
screen image...

CUT TO:

89A   EXT. VAN. TURKEY. COUNTRY. 1915 -- DAY

YOUNG GORKY and SHUSHAN are marching through the desert.
Suddenly, a Turkish soldier on a horse grabs SHUSHAN and

begins to pull her away. YOUNG GORKY grabs her hand and tries to keep her.

CLOSE-UP of the boy's hands tugging at his mother...

CUTS TO:

90   INT. ARSHILE GORKY'S STUDIO. NEW YORK CITY. 1935 -- DAY

GORKY stares at the canvas 'The Artist and His Mother' SHUSHAN's hands are perfectly formed. GORKY, in tears, begins to smudge them out with his bare fingers, then stares at the oil paint on his hands.

ANGLE ON

EDWARD and ROUBEN staring at the screen.

CUT TO:

91   EXT. STUDIO BARN. 1946 -- EVENING

GORKY stands in front of a burning barn, staring into the inferno. He looks at the photograph of his mother and him taken in Van. The light on his face shifts from the colors of the flame to a soft, white light...

CUT TO:

91A   EXT. VAN. TURKEY. STREET. PHOTORAPHER'S AREA. 1912 -- DAY

SEVAN is holding the reflector board in front of GORKY, shining the sunlight into his eyes...

                    CELIA
               (voice over)
          The studio fire destroyed most of
          the canvases he had been working on
          at the time.
               (beat)
          One of the things he saved was the
          photograph of his mother and him.

                    ROUBEN
               (voice over)
          Is this something that was in your
          mind?

                    CELIA
               (voice over)
          When?

CUT TO:

92   INT. DETENTION CENTER -- DAY

ROUBEN is interviewing CELIA. CELIA is completely cool and
obliging.

                    ROUBEN
          When you attacked the painting.
          Were you thinking about all the
          destruction in Gorky's life?

CELIA considers this.

                    CELIA
          Yes. Maybe something in me sensed
          that.

                    ROUBEN
               (impatient)
          Sensed what?

                    CELIA
          That it wasn't supposed to be with
          us. Just like he wasn't. Maybe
          that's why he took his life. He
          didn't feel he was supposed to be
          here.

                    ROUBEN
          Gorky?

                    CELIA
          Gorky. My Dad. Both of them. I
          don't know.

                    ROUBEN
          By trying to destroy the painting,
          don't you think you did even more
          violence to the memory of a man who's
          already suffered way too much?

Pause. CELIA considers this. She is confused.

                    CELIA
          Who are you talking about?

                    ROUBEN
               (suddenly angry)
          I'm talking about one of the greatest
          artists of this century! Don't you
          have any sense of what you tried to
          take away from us?! Don't you feel
          remorse?! Are you happy that the
          painting was restored?
                    (MORE)

>   ROUBEN (CONT'D)
> That it's been saved? Or don't you
> give a fuck?
>   (beat, he calms down)
> What were you feeling when your knife
> went through it?

>   CELIA
> At that moment, I was full of pain.
> I knew that painting was full of
> pain too. I thought that if I
> destroyed it, the pain would stop.

>   ROUBEN
> Did it?

>   CELIA
> Of course not.

                                        CUT TO:

93   INT. TORONTO AIRPORT.   SMALL ROOM -- NIGHT

DAVID is holding one of the canisters. He is about to open
it.

>   RAFFI
> Can we turn out the lights?

>   DAVID
> Why?

>   RAFFI
> So the film won't be ruined.

>   DAVID
> You believe this is film?

>   RAFFI
> Yes.
>   (beat)
> You can feel it in the dark.

>   DAVID
> Alright, Raffi. We'll turn off the
> light.

>   RAFFI
> Thanks.

DAVID turns off the light, plunging the room into complete
darkness.

The heightened sounds of a can being opened over black.

Pause. DAVID speaks in the dark.

                    DAVID
          What do you think I'm touching?

Silence.

                    RAFFI
          Film.

                    DAVID
          You believe that?

                    RAFFI
          Yes.

                    DAVID
          Why?

                    RAFFI
          That's what he told me. That's what
          I need to believe.

                    DAVID
          What would happen if you didn't
          believe it?

                    RAFFI
          I'd be...a criminal.

                    DAVID
          What if I told you it was heroin?

                    RAFFI
          It isn't.

                    DAVID
          Why do you think that?

                    RAFFI
          You would turn the lights on.

                                        CUT TO:

94   INT. TORONTO AIRPORT. ARRIVALS AREA -- NIGHT

ANI rushes into the airport, dressed in her gala evening
costume. She asks an airport security person where she would
receive her son. He points to a direction.

                                        CUT TO:

95   INT. TORONTO AIRPORT. SMALL ROOM -- NIGHT

The lights in the examination room are back on. DAVID is alone.

RAFFI has been let go.

DAVID stares at his hands. There is white powder on his fingers which have touched the mysterious 'film'.

The open canister reveals it is full of drugs.

                            CUT TO:

96   INT. TORONTO AIRPORT. CUSTOMS ARRIVAL AREA -- NIGHT

RAFFI passes through the arrivals door, emotionally exhausted. ANI is waiting for him. She is still dressed for the premiere. Mother and son embrace.

                    PHILIP
                (voice over)
        You let him go?

                    DAVID
                (voice over)
        Yes.

                            CUT TO:

97   EXT. JANET'S HOUSE. -- DAY

PHILIP and DAVID are pulled up in front of JANET's house, ready to pick up TONY.

                    PHILIP
        What was in the cans?

                    DAVID
        Would you believe me if I told you?

                    PHILIP
        What do you mean?

                    DAVID
        Heroin.

                    PHILIP
        No...

                    DAVID
        Film.

                    PHILIP
          I don't get it. You did check the
          cans.

                    DAVID
          One.

                    PHILIP
          What was in it?

DAVID shrugs, smiling at his son.

                    DAVID
          Does it matter?

                    PHILIP
          Dad...

DAVID looks at his son with great affection.

                    DAVID
          I trusted him.

PHILIP is stunned by this.

                    PHILIP
          He was lying to you all night. He
          changed his story.

                    DAVID
          The more he told me, the closer he
          came to the truth. Until he finally
          told it. I couldn't punish him for
          being honest.

                    PHILIP
          But he was smuggling drugs.

                    DAVID
          He didn't think he was.

                    PHILIP
          How do you know?

                    DAVID
          He didn't believe he could do
          something like that.

Pause. PHILIP tries to absorb this.

                    PHILIP
          Dad, what came over you?

                    DAVID
               (brimming with emotion)
          You did, Philip. I was thinking of
          you.

                                        CUT TO:

97A   INT. UNIVERSITY LECTURE HALL -- DAY

A slide image of the island of Aghtamar. ANI is giving the
lecture to a new set of students.

                    ANI
          From the shores of the village, the
          island of Aghtamar was in plain view.
          As a child, Gorky would travel to
          this island with his mother, who
          would show him the detailed carvings
          on the walls of the church...

                                        CUT TO:

98   EXT. TURKEY -- DAY

A video image of the carvings on the walls of the church,
taken by RAFFI.

                    RAFFI
               (voice over on the
                tape)
          I remember you saying that Gorky's
          mother would bring him here when he
          was a little boy...

ANGLE ON

RAFFI is meeting with CELIA in the guest room of the detention
center. He is showing her this video image on the screen of
his digital camera.

                    CELIA
          Why are you showing this to me?

                    RAFFI
          This is where it should have happened.

                    CELIA
          What?

                    RAFFI
          This is the origin. From the memory
          of this place, to the photograph, to
          the sketch, to the painting...

                         CELIA
              I don't understand.

                         RAFFI
              You told me to go there. To put
              something in my heart. If that was
              going to happen, it would have
              happened here.

                         CELIA
              And did it?

                         RAFFI
              No, nothing at all.
                   (beat)
              Celia, you can't imagine how lost I
              was. I was prepared to throw my
              life away.

    Pause. CELIA looks at RAFFI with feeling.

                         RAFFI (CONT'D)
              But last night, as we were in that
              dark room - as I heard him open that
              can - I sensed the presence...

                         CELIA
              The presence of what, Raffi?

                         RAFFI
              His ghost, Celia. I felt his ghost.

    RAFFI smiles at CELIA. He has been transformed.

                                                    CUT TO:

99   INT. UNIVERSITY LECTURE HALL -- DAY

    ANI is projecting the same slides that were seen at the
    beginning of the film. GORKY's photograph with his mother.
    The sketch that is based on the photograph. The magnificent
    painting that emerged. ANI is alone in the hall. She moves
    up to the projection of the slide, placing her hand over the
    light of SHUSHAN's unfinished hand.

                                                    CUT TO:

99A   INT. GAGOSIAN GALLERY. NEW YORK -- DAY

    A retrospective of Arshile Gorky's work. RAFFI is videotaping
    the show with his digital camera. He turns a corner to come
    across his mother standing in front of Gorky's painting.

                        RAFFI
            Mom?

ANI turns around to face her son's lens, the eyes of Gorky
and his mother staring into the camera with her.

                                                CUT TO:

100   EXT. VAN. TURKEY. 1912 -- DAY

An image of YOUNG GORKY and his MOTHER leaving the
photographic studio. The street is full of life, children
playing games, the market full of activity.

Soon, life would never be the same.

The End.

                                        April, 2001

The historical events in this film have been substantiated by holocaust scholars, national archives, and eyewitness accounts, including that of Clarence Ussher.

To this day, Turkey continues to deny the Armenian Genocide of 1915.

Security guard Philip (Brent Carver) stands in front of the Gorky painting.

Philip (Brent Carver, right) and Celia (Marie-Josée Croze) at the museum gallery in front of the Gorky painting.

Celia (Marie-Josée Croze)

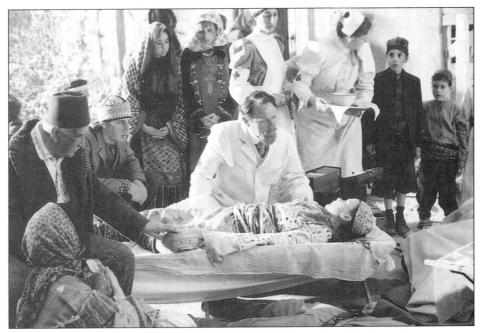

Martin (Bruce Greenwood, center background wearing white coat down on ground) as
  Ussher, trying to save a refugee at the Mission

Unknowingly Ani (Arsinée Khanjian, center foreground) walks into the middle of a scene
  that director Edward Saroyan (Charles Aznavour, seated next to camera wearing dark
  jacket and light blue shirt) is shooting on the Mission set.

Ani (Arsinée Khanjian)

Young Gorky (Garen Boyajian) supporting his mother Shushan Gorky (Lousnak Abdalian, right) in the dessert

A shot of Van burning

Turkish Soldiers (unidentifiable) confront Young Gorky (Garen Boyajian, on right) and Sevan (Haig Sarkissian) in the post-carnage streets of Van.

Unarmed Armenian civilians being tortured by Turkish soldiers in the dessert

Raffi (David Alpay) at Customs after his return from Turkey

Customs Officer David (Christopher Plummer, left) investigates and interrogates Raffi (David Alpay) upon Raffi's return from Turkey.

Customs Officer David (Christopher Plummer)

Ani (Arsinée Khanjian, center left) and Rouben (Eric Bogosian) walk up the theater stairs prior to the premiere screening of *Ararat*.

Martin (Bruce Greenwood, left), Edward (Charles Aznavour, center) and Rouben (Eric Bogosian, right) watch a particularly gruesome scene during the premiere of their film *Ararat*.

Edward (Charles Aznavour) comes through Canadian Customs.

Ani (Arsinée Khanjian)

Raffi (David Alpay, left) and Celia (Marie-Josée Croze) pre-lovemaking

Celia (Marie-Josée Croze, left) and Raffi (David Alpay) post-lovemaking

Raffi (David Alpay, left) and his mother Ani (Arsinée Khanjian)

Ani's (Arsinée Khanjian, pictured in spotlight on stage) art gallery lecture

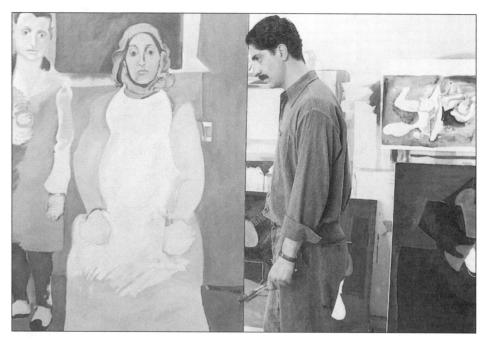

Arshile Gorky (Simon Abkarian) in his studio

Shushan Gorky (Lousnak Abdalian, left, wearing blue flowered apron) and her son Young Gorky (Garen Boyajian, wearing blue topcoat) on their way to the photographer

Young Gorky (Garen Boyajian) and his mother, Shushan Gorky (Lousnak Abdalian)

Shushan Gorky (Lousnak Abdalian) and her son, Young Gorky (Garen Boyajian)

Rouben (Eric Bogosian)

Martin as Ussher (Bruce Greenwood) and Young Gorky (Garen Boyajian, carrying
    American flag) pass through carnage.

A busy street in Van

Edward (Charles Aznavour, left) and Ani (Arsinée Khanjian) on the Mission set

Ali as Jevdet Bey (Elias Koteas)

Ali (Elias Koteas, left) accepts a bottle of champagne from Raffi (David Alpay).

Ali (Elias Koteas)

Atom Egoyan on the set of *Ararat*

AFTERWORD

WATCHING AND TALKING WITH ATOM EGOYAN
BY TIMOTHY TAYLOR

There is a quintessential scene in Atom Egoyan's latest film, *Ararat*. It involves three characters: Ani, an art historian whose book about the Armenian painter Arshile Gorky has been optioned for film; Edward Saroyan, the filmmaker in question, who is mid-way through shooting a movie about the 1915 Armenian genocide; and Martin, the lead actor in Saroyan's film, who plays Dr. Clarence Ussher, a historically factual character, whose diary remains one of the most important records of the tragedy.

Ani has just heard that Gorky's most important painting—one in which the painter's mother is depicted without hands—has been vandalized. The news unsettles her deeply, sparking doubts about her involvement with Saroyan's film. She storms off to speak with Saroyan, and blunders directly onto an active set. The shot she interrupts is taken from the middle of the Turkish siege of the city of Van. Martin, as doctor-hero, spattered in blood, is struggling to save a young child's life. When Ani walks into the middle of this action, demanding that Saroyan speak with her, Martin—who is also Dr. Ussher, who is also the real-life actor Bruce Greenwood—looks up from the carnage and yells at Ani, "What is this? Goddammit! We're surrounded by Turks. We've run out of supplies and most of us will die. This child needs a miracle, this child is bleeding to death!... This is his brother. His pregnant sister was raped in front of his eyes.... His father's eyes were gouged out of his head.... Who the f--- are you?"

Sliding in and out of character, for a moment losing track of which part of his anger should be directed at the on-set intruder, Martin/Ussher/Greenwood stares at Ani as he poses the film's critical question.

The scene lies in the heart of the heart of Egoyan country. Artistic media speak to one another—Gorky's vandalized canvas and Saroyan's ruined shot. Objectivity and voyeurism are nestled. Character is revealed from oblique angles, refracted through other characters. But the scene is also quintessential within the film *Ararat* because, with Martin's question, Egoyan brings all of those involved to a moment of simultaneous self-awareness. This film about genocide pauses to contemplate itself. The director, the actors, and extras, even the audience. The whole constellation of eyes arrayed around this memory of trauma, this film about the memory of trauma, this film within a film about the memory of trauma.

I first encountered the scene in the script, which I read in the summer of 2001, and, as a writer, I was fascinated. *Ararat*, even on the page, felt like the culmination of a body of work to date, bringing together familiar Egoyan themes with the painful details of personal cultural history. But, much further, within that scene, *Ararat* became something I find altogether unusual in cinema these days. The film felt, all at once, like a work that could not have been written by anybody other than Egoyan. This is a quality quite beyond a distinctive style, which most directors can claim in some fashion. Egoyan's work, instead, achieves a sense of full and individual "authorship." And, in that quintessential scene, in the silence following Ussher's challenge, I thought I heard the author contemplating his own question.

Over the course of the next year—watching and talking with Egoyan through production and post—I undertook to find out how he might arrive at an answer.

• • •

Ararat began as a challenge from Egoyan's long-time producer, Robert Lantos. It was delivered in an introduction Lantos gave the filmmaker before a gathering at the Armenian Community Centre in Toronto. Lantos was then beginning production of *Sunshine*—"A film about my people, the Hungarian Jews," he tells me. "So I said, whenever Atom feels that he wants to tell the story that he really has to tell, I will be there to make sure that film is made."

There was a thunderous ovation in response. "We have *Schindler's List*, *The Garden of the Finzi-Continis* and *The Pawnbroker*," Egoyan explains, about the evening. "But nothing similar about the Armenian genocide."

A friendly personal challenge might be considered an unusual launching point for a director whose work has so often been described as cerebral, even dispassionate. But it was the perfect beginning for this particular film. Egoyan—raised in a fully assimilated Armenian family in suburban Victoria, B.C.—came to Toronto in 1978 to study, and became involved in the Armenian Students Association at the University of Toronto. Several years later, during the casting of his first feature film, *Next of Kin*, he met his future wife, Arsinée Khanjian, who, unlike Egoyan, had been raised speaking Armenian and was engaged with the details of her cultural history. During this period, Egoyan had something of a cultural rebirth, one that was manifest in his film *Calendar*. Over 15 years later, when he took the podium after Lantos' challenge, he found himself looking into the expectant face of the Armenian community, into the face of his own awakening as a young man. Into the very face, you might say, of the question: Who are you?

Right there, Egoyan pledged to make the film. And with the completion and release of *Felicia's Journey*, he wrote the *Ararat* script and began to gather his collaborators: regulars, including Khanjian, Greenwood, composer Mychael Danna, and director of photography Paul Sarossy, as well as first timers, including Eric Bogosian and Charles Aznavour. In the summer of 2001, the year-long process of producing this very personal film began.

· · ·

A set, for all the seeming chaos, is a good place to watch people. The environment is so frenetic, the cross currents of so many jobs confluent in such cramped quarters, that there is hardly room for affectation. I arrive on the *Ararat* set in July 2001, when Egoyan is shooting scenes with Khanjian's character, Ani, her son, Raffi (played by first-time actor David Alpay), and Celia, Raffi's stepsister and now lover (played by Marie-Josée Croze).

One of the first things that strikes me about the director's style, on-set, is his overt enthusiasm. He is excited by historical material they've shot. He marvels at the technology that has allowed him to see footage with mocked-up sound the day before. Egoyan, in short, does not act cool on-set, something Eric Bogosian thinks is essentially Armenian. "We're not cold motherf---ers," Bogosian says, about the heritage he shares with Egoyan. "We're warm motherf---ers."

But this is also something that Bogosian believes makes Egoyan unique. Directors, in general, he tells me over breakfast, when we speak, can usually be counted on to be the best actors on-set. They manipulate. They hide their feelings. "A Coppola or an Altman," he says, "they have everybody in the palm of their hands thinking they're these loving, avuncular men. When, in fact, they're very calculatingly moving the whole enterprise forward, step by step. But Atom does something I've never seen any director do, ever. He shows his hand."

We're shooting in a khaki-coloured brick building at the corner of Lowther Avenue and Bedford Road, in Toronto. Inside and outside the house is the typical shambles of the half-made film. Props and gear, reflectors, grip trolleys, a craft-services tent and that particular type of person who work the film trades, a sort of Jimmy Buffett halfway morphed into a carny wearing Blundstones.

Amid this action, Egoyan on-set is an interesting paradox. He is, simultaneously, hyper-focused on what everybody is doing and completely unobtrusive. Depending on what is going on at any given moment, he is either the absolute centre of attention, the person upon whom all eyes are fixed, or he looks like someone who has just wandered onto the set. This latter aspect is prevalent between shots, which is to say, a lot of the time. During these long stretches you might see Egoyan walking slowly from room to room, scanning, thinking about the next moves, staying out of the way.

During shot planning, blocking, and rehearsals, of course, Egoyan assumes command, and a triangle of communication forms between the director, Paul Sarossy, the director of photography (DOP), and the actors. The collaboration between Egoyan and Sarossy is emblematic of the overall approach.

"Paul is completely painting the frame," Egoyan tells me, having given his instructions and, now, stepping back from the action while lights are hung and the camera is positioned for an intimate shot of mother and son in Raffi's bedroom. "I'm really specific about how the frame should look, but I leave the light to him."

In fact, Egoyan tells me, while he knows exactly what he wants and knows the DOP's job well enough to be very specific, he relies on Sarossy to render the idea. When filming *The Adjuster,* he remembers, he thought Sarossy had overlit a particular shot in which they were going for a dark and mysterious feel. "And, of course, what he had done is over-light so he could then shoot with the aperture down and achieve a denser black. I'm quite literal-minded when it comes to seeing what I see. I can't necessarily tell you how this will look on film. That's what he does."

Sarossy, a redhead with a bo'sun's pipe around his neck, is also something of the dry wit on-set. Living in Ireland has given him the cadence of Irish speech, and, when he explains a shot to a dolly operator, he says wryly, "Same again, but more lugubrious." Or, talking to the set decorators, he might say something like, "Remove those beige screens, please, they are competing with the actors."

When the room is lit and the actors are on their marks, the shot is announced and the entire set freezes. The air conditioner shudders to silence. Cellphones are powered down. Grips stand in the stairwell like the crewmen from *Das Boot* waiting for the depth charge. And, at the moment the camera rolls, a bubble of creative pressure seems to shimmer around the director, the camera, and the performers. Egoyan's whole body suggests his focus. He will stand next to the camera, staring intently at some fragment of the action—Khanjian's hand on the sheet or Alpay's face—all the while working his lower lip nervously with the fingers of his left hand. Or he may stand away, head to one side, eyes on the ceiling, listening to the performance. To the words alone.

When the "cut" comes, this bubble dissolves and the room explodes with activity. The still photographer slides into place, snapping his shots. Craft services announces that Popsicles are available outside. The script supervisor scribbles continuity notes in her flip pad. Egoyan watches the video playback with Khanjian and Sarossy, hand again working his lower lip, considering what they have. Deciding if it's what they need.

His work with actors is, in some ways, more subtle, more difficult to evaluate. The flow of directorial advice is almost always sotto voce, Egoyan leaning in close to make eye contact or to say quiet words next to somebody's ear. Of course, direction is personal. No actor wants the director's comments about a performance aired in front of the crew, who will then be in a position to appraise the subsequent take. "When a director directs you," Bruce Greenwood explains, "you're doing it for him. It's between you and him."

But every actor I speak with will agree on one thing. Just as Egoyan is both the centre of attention and unobtrusive on-set, he works with actors in a way that combines a highly articulated vision of what he wants from a character, with a level of collaboration unusual in the industry. In fact, everyone I speak with will tell me he is the most collaborative director they've ever worked with. So consistent is this message, in fact, I might have taken it to be the party line, if it hadn't been repeated in conversation after conversation over the course of a year.

"Atom was very open to my search for the character," Bogosian tells me. "He actually listens, and I know a lot of directors that just kind of humour you and then try to get back to whatever it was they wanted in the first place."

"Atom is actually excited to hear an actor's response to a character," Bruce Greenwood says. "He comes in with the script. You come in with your interpretation. You talk, and it grows from there. I can't really think of another director I've had that with."

Of course, just as words on the page are the mere beginning of things, a conversation about character between actor and director is only a small further addition. A character is created in the unique and unexpected moment captured on film. This point is brought home watching Egoyan direct Arsinée Khanjian. Her character, Ani, whose braininess is based on a particularly smart professor Egoyan had at U of T, is a constant and confident analyzer. In the bedroom shot with her son, Raffi, Egoyan leans in at one point to whisper an idea. Khanjian listens with Ani's sharp-edged focus, processing the private words as Egoyan withdraws to stand in the relative darkness next to Sarossy and the camera. He does not look back at her, even though she stares after him, her expression one of intense calculation, as if she is running the numbers and computing whether an additional piece of data is good news or very bad.

And when they roll, Egoyan stands to one side, eyes on the ceiling, hand on his chin. It strikes me that he is trying to hear right through the words—which have no doubt been dulled by the endless repetition—right through to the motive and intent, the essence of the character that is, just that instant, being created. For each character, in effect, a sub-iteration of the question is posed: Who are you? And it is in these fleeting, filmed moments that the answer is collaboratively spoken.

Khanjian now says her line, the emotional spin of the words minutely adjusted. And when the sequence is complete, the room teeters, waiting for the "cut," and Egoyan twists his body, applying English to the silence, feeling for the moment.

· · ·

The next day, I have a chance to see Egoyan work with a less intimate group. In the scene, a convivial group of Armenians have a drink before a dinner party at Ani's house, and, at a critical moment, her estranged stepdaughter, Celia, appears. It's a typically complex Egoyan shot, with energy sharply changing shape and direction within the space of a few moments.

Egoyan and Sarossy walk the room, visualizing the master shot. Egoyan looks through a loose frame of fingers he holds on either side of his jaw line. "Open to here," he says, spinning and moving backward. "Then pull back. Then over." Sarossy hovers at his shoulder, eye pressed to a viewfinder. Khanjian and the other actors trail behind, all trying to see themselves in the shot.

The imaginary camera does a three-point turn, taking in the entire main floor of the house, capturing Khanjian's character, Ani, negotiating visually between her son and her stepdaughter. There's a second of group silence as the mood of the movement settles into them. "I think that's the shot," Egoyan says, finally.

Of course, it's only the idea of the shot, and much work is required for it to be realized. Now Egoyan withdraws, and the rest of the team springs into action. Props are arranged. The camera crew marks the floor for the dolly. And a discussion about camera axis arises between Sarossy, Khanjian, and the script supervisor.

"Axis is a rule from the birth of cinema," Egoyan explains to me. "Which I've always taken to mean that cinema is the language of dreams. But it's also a part of the process I do not get involved in."

In short, it's a debate about camera positioning. When filming a group of actors (say, four standing in a square, talking) various camera positions are needed to convey the impression of the actors existing together in a comprehensible three-dimensional space. And if the camera crosses an artificial line known as "the axis," you break the viewed reality of the actors being together. In fact, weirdly, if you cross the axis, it can have the effect of making one actor disappear. You lose them, mentally and visually.

Egoyan wanders off to the window. Sarossy and the script supervisor are pivoting back and forth, considering options. Khanjian is standing in various spots by the stairs, trying to visualize herself through the eye of a camera projected onto a screen at some undefined point in the future. Egoyan appears at my elbow again. "You can get insurance for it now, though," he says, straight-faced. "Axis insurance. In case you actually do lose an actor."

And back to the window he goes, hand on his chin.

When Sarossy and his team have set the shot, the Armenian extras are escorted inside where they are arranged in place. Two men stand in the background, fake-grazing a dining-room table covered in Armenian food. Eggplant. Dolma. Kofta. Topig. Kadayif. The living-room extras are poised on couches and chairs. The woman a little stiff. The young men rather purposefully lounging in their assigned spots. "This is tricky," Egoyan whispers. "You have a gathering of Armenians and usually there is this explosive energy. But I can feel people getting nervous."

"Here comes a break in the clouds," someone calls, from the front window.

"Right," Sarossy says, hand on the camera trigger. "Let's shoot that shot."

They get it eventually. The extras relax. They nibble food. After one false start, where everyone on the couch manages to sip their wine at the same instant, they achieve that paradoxical on-camera rhythm where you pay absolutely no attention to something you are doing with mind-bending deliberation. One guy, listening to Alpay recite a poem, ad libs a mocking heartthrob with his hand: pa-pum, pa-pum. Egoyan loves it, shaking his head, smiling as he watches the video. "That was really, really good."

And in the background, just over my shoulder, two crew members—who, as a type, are not known for starry eyes about the film business—are infected by the frank enthusiasm that permeates the set.

"Handsome!" "Yeah, and notice how he framed up those two in the dining room in the back ground? Then: zoot, zoot. Back into the living room. Very cool." "Classic Egoyan, really."

•   •   •

Of course, the shot itself is a fraction of the finished product in any film production. Only, more so in the case of Egoyan, whose stories invariably revolve around complex, multiple timelines and for whom, as a result, editing is an enormously important part of the process of authoring his stories.

"The most vulnerable moment actually comes at assembly," Egoyan tells me, referring to the moment when a rough cut of the film with temporary sound is produced. "All of the mistakes are glaring. All the things that don't work are obvious. And no matter how many times you've been through it before, there's a moment of panic. But, then, the next day you're in the editing room and you start dealing with the issues."

When we meet again, this process is complete. The picture has been locked, although not without surprise adjustments. Scenes between Alpay and Christopher Plummer (who plays a customs agent who's interrogating Raffi on his return from Armenia) have been retooled, to focus on Plummer and his reactions. "When a confession is played out on the face of a person receiving the news, you get an entirely different emotional journey," Egoyan explains, happy with the result.

Now it is time to layer on the sound, which is, again, in Egoyan's case, a complex and critical phase of the process. "The score roots the film," Egoyan has said.

In fact, the work of Egoyan's long-time composer, Mychael Danna, began many months before. "Typically, composers don't get involved until final cut approaches," Danna tells me. "But with Atom, because our relationship goes back so far, I actually read early drafts of the script and we begin discussions at that stage."

And here, again, Danna describes a work relationship that is characterized by both vision and collaboration. "I've never worked with anyone as musically literate as Atom," Danna says. "But Atom also has this unique faith and trust in my work. And when you're trusted, you respond to the absolute highest level of your ability. These are my favourite film experiences."

Danna's completed score combines traditional Armenian melodies with original composition. No simple character themes either. Instead, Danna and Egoyan have crafted a complex musical foundation for the images, based on four pieces of music representing the film's core concepts: the diaspora, the dream of homeland and the abiding notions of Mother and Father. Those themes, plus the late addition of a song by the Armenian punk band System of a Down. A song called "P.L.U.C.K."

"Politically Lying Unholy Cowardly Killers," Egoyan explains, laughing.

Now, at Toronto's Deluxe Studio One—which looks like the NORAD war room with its thousand-dialled console and computer screens and wall-height video playback screen—Egoyan and his sound team are painstakingly fitting score and sound with the filmed action. His editor, Susan Shipton, is here, along with recording mixer Daniel Pellerin, sound designer Steve Munro, and Ross Redfern, who originally recorded the location sound.

The team combs through the frames, tweaking the mix, laying in the foley (non-location sounds, recorded in the studio), adding the sound effects and the music. Every birdsong outside, every gunshot in every battle scene is considered. Every string of spoken words, every passage of Danna's music must be balanced. This has been going on for a month already, and, in the days I watch, only a few minutes of actual film are completed. This despite the fact, Pellerin emphasises, that Egoyan is one of the most organized directors around and makes no picture changes during the mix. If this were a Hollywood film, executives would be hovering at this stage, poring over market-research data and demanding the film be tweaked to meet the demands of test audiences. But here, too, Egoyan the author is evident, standing next to the mixing board, staring up at the playback as the five-second loops of tape are played and replayed. As every brush stroke of sound is painstakingly applied.

• • •

"A film is a summation; it's some part of everything you've been through." Egoyan told me this on-set in July 2001, in our first conversation. In August 2002, I finally get to see the summation.

Now that I have seen the pieces come together, it is immediately clear to me onscreen what movies can do, what is their fundamental power. How, for example, Danna's music can been seen to layer meaning and emotion under the images. How performances seemed louder live than they ultimately do on film. Emotions that seemed overwrought are now smooth with light, with movement, with sound, and with the expanse of a visual narrative stretching around them—as opposed to the shambles of a set.

It is also fascinating to observe, in this particular case, how the film work of Egoyan and his director character, Edward Saroyan, have been starkly differentiated. Personal and idiosyncratic, on the one hand. Epic, formal, even broad, on the other. (Saroyan has Mount Ararat visible from the city of Van, which it is not.) That larger-scale film—with its horrifying scenes of genocide and its glossing of the details in service of the root point—is not as personal a vision, is not authored in the same way as is Egoyan's film, the contemporary drama that sometimes nervously frames the epic.

All this notwithstanding, as a writer, I am biased toward the word. And having read the script—having been introduced to this story with only the bare words spoken by the characters—I find myself now watching the performances most closely, listening for the lines. As Egoyan, the author of those words, has himself told me, "When it's my own material, I see all these characters as having various aspects of my own personality."

And, having been fascinated a year before by a quintessential scene, by the query hovering over that scene and the implied quest for an answer, I am focused when that moment comes, when Martin/Ussher/Greenwood looks up from the carnage of history—gazing up into the past of a Saroyan film in production, through the still more recent past of Egoyan film in production, and right up into the present of the screening in this empty Fifth Avenue theatre in Vancouver—and asks his question: Who are you?

Saroyan's cameras whirr to a stop. His crew members' voices may be heard to complain incredulously at Ani's intrusion. And in the seconds that close the scene, I think I do hear something like an answer from the author, or at least from his onscreen proxies: Ani, Martin, and Saroyan.

Ani reels at her own blunder, realizing all at once what a tiny cog her personal story is in the midst of this enormous project. Realizing, perhaps, that there are limits to what can be understood about history through the sheer exertion of the intellect, of the will. Martin, too, is a participant in the drama. He struggles to separate himself from character, from a terror he has been asked to feel. As Ussher, he is, doubtless, remembering the words of a woman who witnessed the horror and said to him, "How shall I dig out these eyes of mine? Tell me how."

And what of Saroyan, the director of the film-within-a-film? His expression after Ani ruins his shot is both angry and vulnerable. He appears to be asking himself, Indeed, who am I? And what is this film that I have made? Will it communicate the truth? Will it transmit the trauma of history in a way that is beneficial? Or is it a thing of exquisite, but ultimately useless, beauty?

Asked further about his identification with characters in the story, Egoyan told me he identifies most with Raffi, the young man who is transformed by his exposure to the story of his own cultural heritage. Raffi, whose father was a terrorist killed in an assassination attempt and who is torn apart by this aspect of personal history. Reunited with his stepsister, Celia, after a trip he has taken to Mount Ararat, he tells her, "I felt his ghost. The ghost of my father." This statement captures, in effect, who Raffi has decided that he is in the midst of this history and this drama. He is the person, finally, who, through a long journey to the mountain itself, has managed to feel the ghost. To feel it with his hands.

This is near the very end of the film. Saroyan's project is over. Egoyan the filmmaker is firmly back at the helm. In the following scene, as if to punctuate this point, we are shown an audience leaving an auditorium after one of Ani's art-history lectures. And when that fictional audience has left its auditorium, presaging what we, here in the real present, will do in just a few moments, Ani walks over and touches the slide of Gorky's most famous painting: his mother depicted with no hands.

"Gorky's homage to his mother was bound to take on a sacred quality," she told her audience. "His experience as a survivor of the Armenian genocide is at the root of its spiritual power. With this painting, Gorky had saved his mother from oblivion, snatching her out of a pile of corpses to place her on a pedestal of life."

It would seem to me that Atom Egoyan—in a film that touches ghosts and invokes the power of collective memory—has now done something similar.

TIMOTHY TAYLOR is an award-winning writer of both fiction and nonfiction. His bestselling first novel *Stanley Park* was nominated for numerous awards including Canada's prestigious Giller Prize. His second book *Silent Cruise: A Novella and Stories* includes the winners of such awards as the Journey Prize and the National Magazine Award for Fiction. He is presently working on another novel and the screen adaptation of *Stanley Park*.

CAST AND CREW CREDITS

ALLIANCE ATLANTIS and SERENDIPITY POINT FILMS in association with EGO FILM ARTS
present a ROBERT LANTOS PRODUCTION a film by ATOM EGOYAN

ARARAT

DAVID ALPAY   CHARLES AZNAVOUR   ERIC BOGOSIAN   BRENT CARVER   MARIE-JOSÉE CROZE
BRUCE GREENWOOD   ARSINÉE KHANJIAN   ELIAS KOTEAS   AND CHRISTOPHER PLUMMER

Costume Designer BETH PASTERNAK   *Production Designer* PHILLIP BARKER
Editor SUSAN SHIPTON   *Music by* MYCHAEL DANNA   *Director of Photography* PAUL SAROSSY, CSC, BSC
Associate Producers SIMONE URDL and JULIA ROSENBERG   *Co-producer* SANDRA CUNNINGHAM
Produced by ROBERT LANTOS and ATOM EGOYAN   *Written and Directed by* ATOM EGOYAN

Produced with the participation of
TELEFILM CANADA, THE MOVIE NETWORK and SUPER ECRAN,
ASTRAL MEDIA THE HAROLD GREENBERG FUND

Arshile Gorky . . . . SIMON ABKARIAN
Edward . . . . CHARLES AZNAVOUR
David . . . . CHRISTOPHER PLUMMER
Ani . . . . ARSINÉE KHANJIAN
Dinner Guest/Wailing Mother . . . . SETTA KESHISHIAN
Raffi . . . . DAVID ALPAY
Dinner Guest #3/Doctor #1 . . . . SHANT SRABIAN
Celia . . . . MARIE-JOSÉE CROZE
Ali/Jevdet Bay . . . . ELIAS KOTEAS
Philip . . . . BRENT CARVER
Tony . . . . MAX MORROW
Janet . . . . CHRISTIE MacFADYEN
Customs Officer . . . . DAWN ROACH
Young Gorky . . . . GAREN BOYAJIAN
Gorky's Mother . . . . LOUSNAK ABDALIAN
Photographer . . . . RAOUL BHANEJA
Sevan . . . . HAIG SARKISSIAN
Rouben . . . . ERIC BOGOSIAN
Clarence Ussher/Martin . . . . . . BRUCE GREENWOOD
Art Teacher . . . . GINA WILKINSON
Child at Gallery . . . . ARSHILE EGOYAN
Armenian Fighters . . . . KEVORK ARSLANIAN
VIC KESHISHIAN
SERGE KESHISHIAN
ARTHUR HAGOPIAN
GEORGE KHARLAKIAN
SHANT KABRIELIAN
Doctor #2 . . . . VARAZH STEPHEN

Turkish Officer . . . . SAMIR ALNADI
Turkish Soldier . . . . CARLO ESSAGIAN
Translator . . . . ROSE SARKISYAN
Celia's Father . . . . CHRIS GILLETT
Third Assistant Director . . . . JEAN YOON
Wounded Teen Patient . . . SHAHAN BULAT-MATOSSIAN
Teen Patient's Brother . . . . . . MANUEL ISHKHANIAN
German Woman . . . . SUSAN RAYMOND
Armenian Brides . . . . . LORNA NOURA KEVORKIAN
MANDYF NISSANI
MANAL ELMASRI
ROBERTA ANGELICA
ANDREA LOREN
ARAXIE KESHISHIAN
Rape Victim . . . . LINDA GIZIRIAN
Girl Under Cart . . . . . . NICOLE ANOUSH STRANG
Journalist . . . . ERICA EHM

Stunt Performers

JAMIE JONES   RON WEBBER
BILL LINDERS   PAUL RUTLEDGE
BARRY THOMPSON   GUY BEWS
BRENT WOOLSEY   CAM SUTHERLAND
GEORGE JOSEF   CHARLES ANDRE
CORRY GLASS   KIM WIESNER
CATHY SUTHERLAND   WANDA FERRATON
SKYLAR MANTLER   REG GLASS
JOHN DODDS   TOM EIRICKSON
KIRK JARRETT   DAVE VAN ZEYL

First Assistant Director	FERGUS BARNES	Set Dressers	RICHARD FERBRACHE
Second Assistant Director	JOANNE D. MALO		DAVID JAQUEST
Third Assistant Director	GARFIELD RUSSELL	Greens Coordinator	RICHARD SNIDER
Trainee Assistant Director	CINDY IRWIN	Greens Key	TERRY McGAURAN
		Greens Assistant	PETER A. THRASHER
First Assistant Camera	RENI HOZ	Property Master	ALAN DOUCETTE
Second Assistant Camera	DEANNA CADETTE	Lead Props	IMRE de JONGE
Camera Trainees	RENEE PILGRIM	Props Buyer	KATIA de PENA
	JACLYN YOUNG	Military Consultant & Armourer	CHARLES TAYLOR
Stills Photographer	JOHNNIE EISEN	Chief Military Consultants	AL J. VRKLJAN
			DAVE SPENCE-SALES
Video Assist	KENT SABATO	Assistant Costume Designer	SHEILA PRUDEN
		Costume Supervisor	ANN HENSHAW
Script Supervisor	JOANNE HARWOOD	Buyer/Truck Supervisor	CHRISTINE URIAS
		On Set Wardrobe	HEATHER BLURTON
Production Coordinator	JANINE ANDERTON	Extra Supervisor	MIA STURUP
Assistant Production Coordinator	SANDY HYHKO	Wardrobe Assistants	JANE FLANDERS
Assistant to Sandra Cunningham	BRAD FOX		REBECCA VILE
Assistants to Atom Egoyan	MARCY GERSTEIN	Milliner	LOREEN LIGHTFOOT
	TANIA LOEFFLER	Seamstresses	MALCOLM PEARCY
			RITTA KOLEVA
Story Consultant	DAVID FRASER	Costume Cutters	JANICE SKINNER
			ANGELA ELTER
Casting Assistant	JENNY LEWIS		NANCY DASILVA
Extras Casting	ZAMERET KLEIMAN	Costume Breakdown	JOANNE SUGG
Extras Casting Assistant	LOUISA CABIDDU		TRELAWNIE MEAD
			GAYE GARDINER
Sound Recordist	ROSS REDFERN		
Boom Operator	PETER MELNYCHUK	Hair Stylist	VINCENT SULLIVAN
Art Director	KATHLEEN CLIMIE	Assistant Hair Stylist	DIVYO PUTNEY
1st Assistant Art Director	STEPHANIE COLLINS		
Set Designer	PAT FLOOD	Make-up Artist	SYLVAIN COURNOYER
2nd Assistant Art Director	EMIR GELJO	Assistant Make-up Artist	JULIA VALENTE
Research Assistant	ANITA DORON	Prosthetic Make-up Technician	FRANCOIS DAGENAIS
Art Dept. Trainee	ZORKA GOSPAVIC	Location Manager	EARDLEY WILMOT
Gorky Painting Reproductions	ELIZABETH BAILEY	Assistant Location Manager	MALCOLM McCULLOCH
		Location P.A.	JAMES DUFFY
Head Researcher	ARAZ ARTINIAN	Location Security	PETER KENNEDY
Special Thanks to	PROFESSOR		
	DR. VAHAKN N. DADRIAN	Gaffer	DAVID OWEN
		Best Boy Electric	JERRY BORRIS
Construction Coordinator	JIM HALPENNY	Electrics	TOM McGRATH
Head Carpenter	ROB BONNEY		HEINZ GLOSS
Assistant Head Carpenter	STEVE ROMOLO	Generator Operator	HUGH YOUNG
Key Scenic Artist	IAN NELMES	Rigging Gaffer	MARVIN MACINA
Charge Scenic	STEPHANIE YARYMOWICH		
Head Painter	RANDY ROSS	Key Grip	RICO EMERSON
Assistant Head Painter	LAURA MONETA	Best Boy Grip	SEAN BOURDEAU
Head Plasterer	MICHAEL SHERWIN	Dolly Grip	ROBERT COCHRANE
On Set Painter	CHERYL LADRILLO	Grips	STEVE COCKS
			MARTIN LAKE
Set Decorator	PATRICIA CUCCIA	Rigging Grip	ROY ELLISTON
Set Dec Buyer	SHERI O'ROURKE		
Set Dec Lead Man	DAVID DeMARINIS		
On Set Dresser	DAVID EVANS		

Unit Publicist . . . . JOE EVERETT

Production Accountant . . . . IRENE PHELPS
First Assistant Accountant . . . . ANNE JURENAS-POLYAK
Second Assistant Accountant . . . . . . DARREN WILSON
Post Production Accountant . . KATMADHU PRODUCTIONS

Special Effects Coordinator . . . . JORDAN CRAIG,
PERFORMANCE SOLUTIONS
Shop Coordinator . . . . DEBBIE GALLANT
Special Effects Key . . . . ALI MURVA
Animal Wrangler . . . . RICK PARKER
Stunt Coordinator . . . . JAMIE JONES

Transport Coordinator . . . . WILFRED C. BELL
Transport Captain . . . . MARK VAN ALSTYNE
Set Dec Driver . . . . JOHN IGNAGNI
Head Driver . . . . JIM BEAUDROW
Drivers . . . . JOHN COCKS
RUDY BACCUCHI
BRUCE RAYMER
Honeywagon . . . . KEN GROOMBRIDGE
Transport Security . . . . PATRICK BENSON

Armenian Translations . . . . . . MANUEL KEUSSEYAN
Historic Consultant . . . . GREG CHOPOORIAN
Dialogue Coach . . . . FRANÇOIS GRISÉ
Acting Coach . . . . BRUCE CLAYTON
Production Assistant . . . . MICHELLE BERRIGAN
Assistant to Mr. Aznavour . . . . SARO AYNEDJIAN
Director Observer . . . . . . WIEBKE VON CAROLSFELD
Consultant to Mr. Plummer . . MYROCIA WATAMANIUK
Education Liaison . . . . LAUREL BRESNAHAN
Tutors . . . . PATSY McVICARS
LAURIE FARRANCE

Caterer . . . . BY DAVIDS'
Craft Service . . . . STARCRAFT SERVICES INC.
On Set Craft . . . . JODY CLEMENT
KIMSHA HORVATH

Post Production Supervisor . . . . DOUGLAS WILKINSON

First Assistant Editor . . . . MICHELE FRANCIS
Second Assistant Editor . . . . . . CHAD GLASTONBURY
Apprentice Editor . . . . MARK GRIFFIN

Sound Editing Facility . . . . TRACKWORKS INC.
Dialogue Editor . . . . DAVID DRAINIE TAYLOR
Sound Effects Editor . . . . KEN CADE
ADR Editor . . . . SUSAN CONLEY
Assistant Sound Effects Editor . . . . COLIN BAXTER
Assistant Dialogue Editor . . . .
TIMOTHY W. MEHLENBACHER
Assistant Sound Editor . . . . PETER KAMBASIS

Loop Group Coordination . . . . . SETTA KESHISHIAN
THE CALDWELL AGENCY
Supervising Re-Recording Engineer . . DANIEL PELLERIN
Re-Recording Engineers . . . . PETER KELLY
ANDREW TAY
Re-Recording Assistants . . . . BRENT MacLEOD
MATT CLUET

Foley Artists . . . . ANDY MALCOLM
GORO KOYAMA
Foley Record Mixers . . . . RON MELLEGERS
DON WHITE
Foley Record Assistants . . . . REBECCA WRIGHT
MARIANA GAVRILESCU
FUMIKO KOYAMA
Foley Recording Studio . . . . FOOTSTEPS SOUND
ADR Recording Engineers . . . . GREG SHIM
DAVE YONSON
BRENT ROACH

Visual Effects . . . . MR. X INC., TORONTO
Visual Effects Supervisor . . . . DENNIS BERARDI
Visual Effects Producer . . . . SYLVAIN TAILLON
Compositing Supervisor . . . . AARON WEINTRAUB
Digital Matte Artist . . . . KRISTY BLACKWELL
3D Animators . . . . DAVE CALDER
DONG YON KANG
Visual Effects Compositor . . . . . MARCO POLSINELLE
Visual Effects Coordinator . . . . . . MATTHEW STEVES
Software Developer . . . . COLIN WITHERS

Negative Cutting . . . . FRANCONT FILM
Head Title Design . . . . JOHANNA WEINSTEIN
Film Timer . . . . CHRIS HINTON
Titles by . . . . FILM EFFECTS INC.
Subtitles and Opticals by . . FILM OPTICALS OF CANADA

Orchestration . . . . NICHOLAS DODD
MYCHAEL DANNA
Conductor . . . . NICHOLAS DODD
Score Mixed by . . . . BRAD HAEHNEL
Music Editor . . . . PAUL INTSON
Orchestra Contractor . . . . ISOBEL GRIFFITHS
Leader . . . . JOHN BRADBURY
Copyist . . . . VIC FRASER
Assistants to the Composer . . . ANDREW LOCKINGTON
APARNA BHARGAVA
Score Produced by . . . . MYCHAEL DANNA
Music Research . . . . EVE EGOYAN

Orchestra Recorded & Mixed at . . . .
AIR STUDIOS (LYNDHURST) LONDON

ISABEL BAYRAKDARIAN, Soprano
Recorded at . . . GLENN GOULD STUDIO, TORONTO
Engineer . . . . RON SEARLES

Armenian Choir

ARTSVI BAKHCHINYAN   SARGIS KHARAZYAN
MKRTICH KUBELYAN   ARTUR MANOUKYAN
TIGRAN STAMBOLTSYAN   HRAYR TATIKYAN
SARGIS TOROSSYAN   DEREN VARDOUMYAN

Choir recorded at
The Church of Saint Gayane, Etchmiadzin, Armenia

Armenian Folk Musicians
GEVORK DABAGHIAN - duduk, zurna
GRIGOR TAKUSHIAN - dham duduk
KAMO KHACHATURIAN - dhol
LEVON TEVANIAN -shvi, tav shvi
ARTYOM KHACHATURIAN - tar
KARINE HOVHANNISIAN - kanon
TIGRAN AMBARIAN - kamancha
NORAYR KARTASHIAN - bhul ney

Recorded at Argo Studio, Yerevan, Armenia
Production Coordinator . . . . ANDRANIK MICHAELIAN
Recording Engineer . . . . STEPAN BEROOJANIAN

ALBERT VARDANYAN -
duduk ARTO TUNCBOYACIYAN - saz
Recorded at Casa Mia, Toronto

With thanks to
HAROLD HAGOPIAN, Traditional Crossroads
HARMIK GRIGORIAN, L'Atelier Grigorian,
Rev. SHAHÉ TANOSSIAN, SARKIS HAMBOYAN

Alberta Crew
Production Manager . . . . JANINE ANDERTON
Consultant . . . . DAVID WEBB
Production Coordinator . . . . . KIM GODDARD-RAINS
Assistant Production Coordinator . . . BARBARA CHISHOLM
Trainee Coordinator . . . . JANET STEPHEN
Assistant Accountant . . . . JILL ANTAL

Third Assistant Director . . . . . MATTHEW KERSHAW
Trainee Assistant Director . . . . . PIERRETTE PRETTY
Production Assistants . . . . ANTHONY HART
                                        RICK KRAMER
                                        JOHN KERR
                                        DOUG PIEPGRASS
                                        TROY RUDOLPH
                                        STUART BECKER

'B' Camera Operator . . . . CAM MacDONALD
First Assistant 'B' Camera . . . . . DEAN STINCHCOMBE
Second Assistant 'B' Camera . . . . . . SCHANE GODON
Camera Trainee . . . . BRENT BARRETTE
Video Playback . . . . DAVE JOSHI
Extras Casting . . . . ALYSON LOCKWOOD
Extras Casting Assistant . . . . SUZY GIONETTE

Best Boy Electric . . . . MARTIN KEOUGH
Electrics . . . . MICHAEL GOULD
                                        TONY SKAPER

Generator Operator . . . . ANDREW THOM
Best Boy Grip . . . . JOHN ADSHEAD
Grips . . . . COREY LEE
                                        TIM MILLIGAN

Assistant Set Decorator . . . . ROBIN SWIDERSKI
Lead Man . . . . TOM EDWARDS
On Set Dresser . . . . CHRIS SMITH
Set Decorator Trainee . . . . CHRIS McCRAE
Assistant Greens . . . . TOM YAREMKO

Assistant Props . . . . DEAN GOODINE
                                        LAURIE DOBBIE
Gun Handlers . . . . PRO-LINE SHOOTERS

Construction . . . . F&D SCENE CHANGES
                                        KIRSTY NEILL
On Set Carpenter . . . . BRIAN CAMERON
Scenic Painter . . . . MICHAEL HENTGES

Truck Costumer . . . . KAREN CHRISTENSEN
Background Costume Coordinator . . . .
                                        MICHELLE JOHNSTON
Background On Set Supervisor . . . . . CAROLYN DEVINS
Breakdown . . . . SUSAN MONTALBETTI
Breakdown Costumer/Milliner . . . . JILL FRY
Costumers . . . . COLLEEN BRYANT
                                        NANCY PREVOST
                                        WAUNITA SIMMONS

First Assistant Hair . . . . HEATHER INGRAM
First Assistant Make up . . . . JOANNE PREECE

Location Manager . . . . ROBERT HILTON
Assistant Location Manager . . . . PETER HORN
Location Security . . . . PETER GURR

Stunt Coordinator . . . . GUY BEWS

Animal Wrangler . . . . T.J. BEWS

Paramedics . . . . PRODUCTION PARAMEDICS
                                        DARRYL ARMSTRONG
                                        TANYA HILL
                                        SAMANTHA HUGHES

Transport Coordinator . . . . COLEMAN ROBINSON
Transport Captain . . . . RAY BRECKENRIDGE

Caterer . . . . FILM WORKS CATERING LTD.
Craft Service . . . . CONNIE HOUSE
Assistant Craft . . . . SHIRLEY IRVINE
MARTY ARTHUR

For Serendipity Point Films
Business and Legal Affairs . . . . . . MARK MUSSELMAN
Accounting and Finance . . . . AIDA TANNYAN
Marketing and Publicity . . . . WENDY SAFFER
Assistants to Robert Lantos . . . . . . CHERRI CAMPBELL
KELLY WILLSON HARVEY
Project Coordinator . . . . AMY GREEN
Assistant to Mark Musselman . . . . . . MARIA CARBONE
Assistant Aida Tannyan . . . . . ANGELINA GIACOMINO
Production Assistant . . . . MARC LEFLER

For Alliance Atlantis
Director, Business and Legal Affairs . . . .
ELIZABETH MacFARLANE
Director, Business and Legal Affairs . . . . BRENDA BLAKE
Head of Production . . . . LACIA KORNYLO
Production Executive . . . . ANDREW ROSEN

Raffi's digital video footage shot by
Hrair Hawk Khatcherian, Summer, 2000

The Producers wish to thank
Nouritza Matossian for allowing her book
"Black Angel: A Life of Arshile Gorky" to appear in ARARAT
as the book written by Ani.

English translation of "The Dance"
by Siamanto (Atom Yarjanian)
Courtesy of Peter Balakian from his book
"Bloody News From My Friend: Poems by Siamanto"

"A Mother's Heart" by Avetik Issahakian translated into English

"An American Physician in Turkey: A Narrative of Adventures
in Peace and War" by Clarence Douglas Ussher, 1917

ART

All works by Arshile Gorky: © 2001 Estate of Arshile
Gorky/Artists Rights Society (ARS), NY

"The Artist and His Mother"

Courtesy of the Whitney Museum of American Art, New
York, NY

"Self Portrait"
Courtesy of the Los Angeles County Museum of Art
Gift of Mr. & Mrs. Hans Burkhardt

"Portrait of Vartoosh"
Hirshhorn Museum and Sculpture Garden, Smithsonian
Institution Gift of the Joseph H. Hirshhorn Foundation, 1966

Photo of Arshile Gorky in his studio
By Alexander Sandow

Project SAVE Armenian Photograph Archives

Thanks to
MICHÈLE HALBERSTADT and LAURENT PÉTIN
LARRY GAGOSIAN

HRANT ALIANAK	ARIS BABIKIAN
PETER BALAKIAN	LIZ BALKUM
RUSSELL BANKS	KEVORK BARDAKJIAN
RICHARD BLACKBURN	JACK BLUM
AMNON BUCHBINDER	SHARON CORDER
GARTH DRABINSKY	NIV FICHMAN
CAMELIA FRIEBERG	MARC GLASSMAN
JOEL GREEN	BILL HOUSE
ISABEL KAPRIELIAN	ASTRIG KASHKARIAN
JAMES M. KESHISHIAN	SETTA KESHISHIAN
BILL KROHN	LISA SANDOW LYONS
MARIE-CHRISTINE LUDET	DON McKELLAR
NOURITZA MATOSSIAN	SIS NERCESSIAN
BARBARA MERGUERIAN	CREG SANDOW
MICHAEL ONDAATJE	LEONARD B. ROSMAN
PATRICIA ROZEMA	BARET SARMAZIAN
SOSSY TACHJIAN	RUTH THOMASIAN
GEORGE F. WALKER	STEVEN ZAILLIAN

SUSAN LIN-SYNANIAN &
RICHARD SYNANIAN, ALMA

THE RED CROSS

PAUL SMITH MENSWEAR

GEORGES YEREMIAN &
THE ARMENIAN RUGS SOCIETY

YUMI ETO DESIGNS

INTERNATIONAL FINE FOODS

THE ARMENIAN COMMUNITY CENTRE, TORONTO

FREDERICK SAYADIAN AT AGBU

ARA RUN AT EXCLUSIVE DIAMONDS

THE TOWN OF DRUMHELLER, DARWIN DURNIE

TORONTO FILM & TELEVISION OFFICE,
CITY OF TORONTO

LIBRAIRIE ORIENTALE H. SAMUELIAN - PARIS

LIBRAIRIE NOUBAR PASHA – PARIS

CONGREGAZIONE ARMENA
MECHITARISTA – VENICE

SONGS

Gorky's Music: E. Boghosian, Gulazian's Orchestra
Harsin Dourkin, Gnig Goozem
Pharos Label, NY, NY 1920

"Mystery"
Written by: Gordon Downie and Atom Egoyan
Performed by: Gordon Downie
From the album: "Coke Machine Glow"
Courtesy of Wiener Art Records - copyright 2000
Copyright 2000 - Wiener Art (SOCAN)/Egoyan Ego Film
Arts (SOCAN)

"P.L.U.C.K."
(Politically Lying, Unholy, Cowardly Killers.)
Performed by SYSTEM OF A DOWN
Written by: Malakian/Tankian/Odajian/Dolmayan
DDevil Music (ASCAP)/ System of Down (ASCAP)/ Sony/
ATV Tunes LLC.
All rights on behalf of DDevil Music, System of A Down &
Sony/ ATV Tunes LLC.
Administered by SONY/ ATV Music Publishing,
8 Music Square West, Nashville, TN 37202
All rights reserved. Used by Permission.

Produced With the Assistance/Participation of
CANADA THE CANADIAN FILM OR
VIDEO PRODUCTION TAX CREDIT

THE GOVERNMENT OF ONTARIO

ONTARIO FILM AND TELEVISION TAX CREDIT

Insurance . . . . JONES BROWN & ASSOC. LTD.
Completion Bond . . . . FILM FINANCES CANADA
(1998) LTD.
Payroll Services . . . . . ENTERTAINMENT PARTNERS
CANADA
Avid Provided by . . . . THEATRE D DIGITAL
Post Production Lab . . . . DELUXE TORONTO
Filmed on . . . . KODAK STOCK
Camera Equipment Provided by . . . . PANAVISION®
Equipment Provided by . . . . . WILLIAM F. WHITE LTD.
Filmed at . . . . TORONTO FILM STUDIOS

No animals were harmed during the
production of this motion picture.

www.serendipitypoint.com

www.egofilmarts.com

ABOUT THE FILMMAKER

Writer/Director **ATOM EGOYAN** is a celebrated filmmaker worldwide. His acclaimed adaptation of the Russell Banks novel *The Sweet Hereafter* received two Academy Award® nominations (Best Director, Best Adapted Screenplay) and won both the Grand Prize of the Jury and the International Critics Prize at the Cannes Film Festival. Egoyan's recent features include *Felicia's Journey* and *Exotica*. Cairo-born, Canadian-bred, and of Armenian descent, Egoyan lives in Toronto, Canada, with his wife, actress Arsinée Khanjian, and their son.